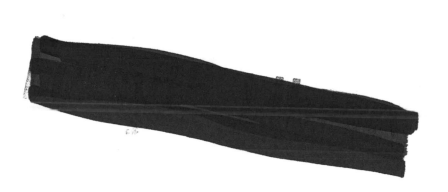

BECKETT, NABOKOV, NIN

Kennikat Press
National University Publications
Literary Criticism Series

BECKETT, NABOKOV, NIN

Motives and Modernism

SYLVIA PAINE

National University Publications
KENNIKAT PRESS // 1981
Port Washington, N.Y. // London

Manufactured in the United States of America

Published by
Kennikat Press Corp.
Port Washington, N.Y. / London

Library of Congress Cataloging in Publication Data
Paine, Sylvia, 1946–
    Beckett, Nabokov, Nin: motives and modernism.

    (Literary criticism series) (National university
publications)
    1. American literature–20th century–History and
criticism. 2. Modernism (Literature) 3. Beckett,
Samuel, 1906– –Criticism and interpretation.
4. Nabokov, Vladimir Vladimirovich, 1899–1977–
Criticism and interpretation. 5. Nin, Anais,
1903–1977–Criticism and interpretation. I. Title
PS228.M63P3   810'.9'005   81-5971
ISBN 0-8046-9288-2   AACR2

For N.

ACKNOWLEDGMENTS

Thanks to Dr. William Wasserstrom for seeing this project through from beginning to end. And, to the following, permission to use copyrighted material is gratefully acknowledged:

Grove Press, Inc., for extracts from *Fizzles*, by Samuel Beckett, copyright © 1976 by Samuel Beckett; *The Unnamable* (from *Three Novels*), by Samuel Beckett, copyright © 1955, 1956, 1958 by Grove Press, Inc.; *Proust*, by Samuel Beckett, all rights reserved, first published 1931; *Poems in English*, by Samuel Beckett, copyright © 1961 by Samuel Beckett; *Samuel Beckett*, by Richard N. Coe, copyright © 1964 by Richard N. Coe, revised 1968.

Véra Nabokov, for extracts from *The Gift*, by Vladimir Nabokov, copyright © 1963 by G. P. Putnam's Sons; *Speak, Memory*, by Vladimir Nabokov, copyright © 1960, 1966 by Vladimir Nabokov; copyright to *The Gift* and *Speak, Memory*, are held by Véra Nabokov.

Gunther Stuhlmann, Author's Representative, for extracts from *Seduction of the Minotaur*, by Anais Nin, copyright © 1961 by Anais Nin, all rights reserved; *Collages*, by Anais Nin, copyright © 1964 by Anais Nin, all rights reserved. Both titles are available in an edition by The Swallow Press, Chicago.

The Swallow Press, for extracts from *A Woman Speaks*, ed. Evelyn J. Hinz, copyright © 1975 by Anais Nin.

Macmillan Publishing Company, for extracts from *The Novel of the Future*, by Anais Nin, copyright © 1968 by Anais Nin.

The Colston Research Society, for extracts from "Metaphor and Symbol," by D. G. James, published in *Metaphor and Symbol*, Colston Paper No. 12, 1960.

CONTENTS

PREFACE

I began this study hoping to find out why literature matters so much, how it works its magic, what makes it usually more compelling than any invitation to do something else. As I considered books in general and the books I love in particular, I realized that their words matter because they speak to the matter in me, because they have the force of physical presence. Yet they also transcend matter, taking me with them. Like other forms of art, literature evokes our sensuous experiences, but it does not stop there. It explores their peripheries and beyond. As Hugh Kenner writes, "Art lifts the saying out of the zone of the things said." The motives for reading seem very like the motives for writing: to discover (or invent) what lies beyond the textures, colors, sounds, scents, and tastes of the surface of life, to achieve the fullest realization of the senses.

This notion is so fundamental to the process of writing that it is universal. I have limited my study to three writers in order to pay close attention to the working of the process which, of course, is unique in each. I have chosen to study modernist writers because the preoccupation with self in this century has brought sensation and the body to the foreground of literature. At the same time, as old forms of religion wane the need is felt to forge a new faith, one that can accommodate yet overcome the limitations of sensory experience and not only justify change and decay but exalt them as a source of the wonder and pain that spark creative energy. Modernist art assumes this spiritual and moral role.

Chapter 1 looks at the unity of the two moving forces of art, the sensuous and the transcendent. Chapter 2 focuses on the unresolvable tension between those forces in Samuel Beckett's puzzling works, especially his late collection *Fizzles*. For Beckett's characters, the contradictions of sense and the longing for transcendence are a predicament, a source of anguish and frustration. In eight short pieces, *Fizzles* shows the monotony of Beckett's concerns but also the gamut of his approaches in his comic-tragic attempt to eliminate the problem. The only "solution" is to fail—to endure, to go on—but, given expression in art, the willingness to fail becomes a form of compassion.

The magic of Vladimir Nabokov's brilliant novels, discussed in chapter 3, distills sense experience into an essence that art explores and expands via imagination until it seems to yield the secret of nature and of creation itself, consciousness magnified by the mirror of art and the mutual reflection of minds in the word. Anais Nin's very different process of transformation, the subject of chapter 4, centers on a struggle for wholeness against the tyranny of self-delusion—a rite beginning in the dark world of dreams and growing toward life and the abundance of feeling that joins love and art, a fruition realized in her novel *Collages*.

Finally, the brief conclusion looks at art as the shared passion of writer and reader, a force that endows art with a spiritual imperative and makes it the sacrament of human understanding in modernist times.

BECKETT, NABOKOV, NIN

Sylvia Paine has taught college English and is presently a writer on the arts for a daily newspaper, *The Forum,* in Fargo, North Dakota. She received her Ph.D. in English from Syracuse University. Besides countless newspaper articles, she has written nonfiction and reviews in *Minnesota Monthly, North Dakota Horizons, Dakota Arts Quarterly,* and the *WARM Journal.*

CHAPTER ONE

INTRODUCTION

...what lies beyond the strictly observable, measurable and verifiable aspects of things? What lies behind the coloured shapes and felt surfaces of things, beyond what is in strictness seen and felt, what can be measured and verified? What are things, natural and human alike, in their inner, impalpable, unseen being? What are things, to use an honoured phrase, and employed extensively by one of the greatest philosophers, what are "things in themselves?" ...The answer is we do not know, and have no way of finding out.... Brought thus sharply to the boundaries of demonstrable, i.e. scientific, knowledge of the world, we are confronted by the illimitable, unplumbed world lying beyond the narrow scope of the discourse of science and the understanding, and in the face of this metasensual world, the world as it is in itself, the unknown being of things, we are left to wonder and surmise; it is from this wonder and surmise that philosophy and art alike take their origin....

—D. G. James, "Metaphor and Symbol"

The artist walks the same earth we all walk, but he meets us in a different world, one that is familiar yet extraordinary, an exaltation or intensification of what we see, feel, and think every day. Art takes root, as D. G. James says, in that wonder and surmise with which an artist confronts the limits of his sensuous perceptions and imagines what lies beyond, what gives his perceptions meaning, what makes them matter. Art becomes metasensual in arranging these familiar, sensuous appearances so as to elicit private secrets and public intimacies and transcendent meanings. Appearances become the

3

instruments of organization, of depth perception, and their unique arrangement enables the artist, using his own individuality (perception, imagination, understanding) to surpass and metamorphose himself. Art of this order
liberates, therefore, but it does not evade. It offers no escape from the self,
from the mind or the body, only the possibility, implicit in the nature of the
creative imagination, of a release—an expansion and evolution and extension in art.

Because the realm of art is that of the imagination, art can arrange and
combine and alter appearances in startling ways, but it cannot discard them,
for they are the very rudiments of imagination. Thus, though free of *this* time
and space, art is not free of time and space altogether: their conjunction
defines the appearances where imagination begins. Poetry (as a generic term
for art or, more specifically, for literature, the form of art with which we are
most concerned here) "is of imagination *all* compact," James writes. "As a
free and autonomous activity of the soul it must remain human and secular;
its end is to imagine, in the form of the symbols it creates, a human and
natural world." And yet that world imagined transcends this world as the
soul transcends the man.

Despite the metaphysical yearnings implicit in its creation, a work of art
itself is subject to physical laws; it assumes an appearance, becomes part of
an age, a place. But art turns these accidents of birth into instruments of
reincarnation, its temporal and sensuous reality, sublimated with feeling and
understanding, coming to life across all the ages, transcending time and
space by giving those dimensions a form in which to endure.

A longing for transcendence and liberation lies at the soul of the artistic
impulse, and it implies a kind of dissatisfaction with the world as created, or
at least with the self as it relates to the created world. The motivation to
create betrays a desire to expand upon the given, to discover its secrets, to
correct its flaws—to master it, to master oneself. This last item is the key
problem, especially in modernist writing: how not only to control but to
make sense of a longing for life and for permanence, contained in a body that
decays and dies. Art, which both asks this question and plays at answering it,
is an emblem of man's predicament—a physical thing which no physical
function, no practical consideration, can explain. Yet there it sits, meaning
something and trying to explain life itself.

If art is the product of man's predicament, his lack of unity within, his lack
of understanding beyond himself, then it follows that a race reconciled to its
nature and to the reality of things external to itself would not need to create
art. All would be harmony. But surely it is true that art is at least part of the
solution to man's predicament in that it calls into being and harmonizes all its
own elements; thus, it provides a metaphor for man's possible evolution, his
vision of the unity of body, mind, and spirit. Further, art expands the

imagination, combines things newly, enlarges the realm of the perceivable, so that both artist and audience feel an increase of freedom within their human limits. Liberation of the human faculties within these limits is the ideal, the ultimate end of art; for as an agent of freedom, art can change life.

Within the scope of imagination man is indeed free, and the scope widens as imagination is given play. It is wide when man imagines himself free, an act that liberates body and mind to mutual service instead of servitude. For as much as they limit each other, they also complement and intensify each other. Functions of the nervous system, the senses bridge body and mind and thereby serve as the primary stage of perception, which diffuses into consciousness—that "decompression of being," as Jean-Paul Sartre called it. Further, man conceives of consciousness diffusing, or decompressing, into a spirit through which he participates, both abstractly and concretely, in being itself. But this progressive diffusion of the faculties of the self does not blur man's physical nature. It makes the body radiant, for the spirit con-volves with the senses, and their experiences become analogous. As Dante's earthly image of Beatrice parallels his heavenly vision of her, so does the body provide a means (the only means given man's mortal condition) of spiritual expression. In *The Name and Nature of Poetry* A. E. Housman says, "If I were obliged to name the class of things to which [poetry] belongs, I should call it a secretion."

Since the senses serve as a primal form of knowing, uniting body, mind, and spirit, liberation of the senses is paramount to human liberation. In *Life against Death* Norman O. Brown—who in this respect conforms to religious belief—makes resurrection of the body a symbol for healing of the spirit. Art invokes the senses in two principal ways, both overt and implicit. In literature the body is recalled through sensuous impressions, description and detail, images and symbols. More subtly, between the reader and the work an intimacy develops of the sort Roland Barthes posits in *The Pleasure of the Text*, where he claims the text is "an anagram of the body . . .of our erotic body."

It is easy to understand the sensuous nature of a novel like *Tom Jones*, for example, which celebrates pleasure (while ostensibly pointing out its dangers) and acknowledges the body's place within the restraints of the social order; or in *Lady Chatterley's Lover*, where sensation is so powerful it defies and even threatens order. It is equally easy to recognize sensuousness in the poetry of the Romantics, for whom sensing nature's impressions, as Wordsworth said, made men "more prompt / To hold fit converse with the spiritual world." Literature of social concern, even ideological writing, draws on the senses to persuade the reader through empathy to appreciate the characters' plight.

But if concrete writing is sensuous, so is even the most abstract art. In fact, abstraction may startle the senses into heightened awareness, as does modern painting, defying our customary intellectual approach, habits of thought, and preconceptions of what art should be. Modern poetry and novels that depart from traditional form and structure can subjugate the reader's intellect (at least initially) and make a fairly direct and sensuous impact—if, that is, the reader is willing to live with some perplexity and does not let it lead him either to a too-strict analysis or away from the text altogether. Instead he must enact the text within the space of his body, as any act of reading requires; for, as Cary Nelson puts it in *The Incarnate Word,* "To read is to draw the world into the body's house." The body is the warm presence welcoming the stranger-text; only thus does the text live and, in turn, nurture the reader.

For both writer and reader, then, art is a source of pleasure—even of erotic pleasure, implicit in the intimacy between author and text, reader and text, author and reader, each engendering new images in the other, becoming the other. Barthes calls the text, which both writer and reader share, a site of bliss affording "the possibility of a dialectics of desire." Reading readily lends itself to an analogy with sexual passivity, the reader penetrated— perhaps even violated—by the language of the text. But reading also has its aggressive side. Geoffrey Hartman notes in "The Fate of Reading" that the very presence of a powerful work of art awakens "our own quasi-daemonic drive for an erotic or envious possession of other lives."

Both aspects of the sensuous nature of art—its evocation of the senses and the intimacy of artist, audience, and work—are, in a special sense, erotic. I am using eroticism as Freud did in calling it the life instinct. Besides this, in eroticism is a fascination with the unknown and the desire to know it—in the Biblical sense—by uniting with it. As Brown says in *Love's Body,* "To heal is to make whole, as in wholesome; to make one again; to unify or to reunify: this is Eros in action. Eros is the instinct that makes for union, or unification." In this definition the sexual in particular and the sensuous in general are only the epicenter of full eroticism, only the physical metaphor for the metaphysical phenomenon. The "essence of eros," says Richard Howard in his introduction to the English translation of Barthes's *S/Z,* is "what is inexpressible." One reason for this inexpressibility is that, although everyone has the five senses, the nature of each individual's sensuous experience is finally unique and private. A more important reason, however, is that the senses are man's connection with nature, the world of matter whose ultimate reality is still outside his ken. Scientifically or physiologically we may understand the senses, and philosophically we may explain them, but ontologically they remain incomprehensible. So close to the mysterious source of being, they are indeed inexpressible.

Paradoxically, the senses participate in both the relativity of private experience and the absolute of being itself, and this apparent contradiction also makes expression impossible, for any attempt to express may, for the sake of logic, either ignore one dimension or exclude so much that it is finally nonsense. What remains unspoken in the spoken word is what makes the word make sense and engenders a potential movement beyond sense, a transcendence—the metasensual. Further, the totality which is the amalgam of relativity and the absolute is equally everything and nothing: the circle may be a zero, depending on one's point of view.

But the artist does not shrink from the inexpressible. As Samuel Beckett says, the artist finds his creativity in the very dilemma that "there is nothing to express, nothing with which to express, together with the obligation to express." In dealing with life, the artist perforce explores the inexpressible which is the erotic essence and origin of all life, that which lies beyond the appearances perceived by the senses yet which is also part of those appearances. For human nature itself is inexpressible; and the strange, compelling life force within it makes man more than a body containing a mind. He is sensual and more. He knows the world through his senses; he feels his senses with his mind as well as with his body—he is conscious of them; and he intuits their meaning. Metasensuality is more concrete than spirit, however, more diffuse than consciousness, more sublime than the body. It is the liberation of all these faculties. Liberation does not, of course, mean libertinism, nor does it mean separation, but freedom from the confines and compartmentation of the self. That is, we are bound to be selves—that is our mortal condition—but we are not thereby diminished, for we discover within the self the reaches of human knowledge, feeling, understanding. It is the senses that make sense of these abstractions, that make them live.

In the work of Samuel Beckett, Vladimir Nabokov, and Anais Nin, a main tendency of modernism is seen with intense clarity. Concentrating, focusing on human sensation, they prefer not to confine the human body within a fairly controlled social structure as earlier writers often did. Like many other modernists who celebrate the body's freedom, they are absorbed in trying to explore fully the role of the senses in advancing the process of self-transcendence.

Every artist, of course, manifests his extrasensory dream and his version of sensuous reality in a unique way. He may, using the senses as the perimeter, voyage inward or outward or nowhere at all in trying to fathom man and nature. Although the artists chosen to illustrate the uses of libera-tion, the ethics and aesthetics of sensuality—Beckett, Nabokov, and Nin—move in different patterns, nonetheless they do share a vision and a sense of human possibility which is social and aesthetic, spiritual and moral. Anais

Nin, scrutinizing the inner self, and Vladimir Nabokov, studying the world beyond the self, both elaborate an ethic of love and responsibility which is self-transcendent, which generates art and is generated by the senses. Samuel Beckett, caught in the impossibility of knowing either world, derives a sort of courage which is the essence of liberation in that it transcends the will, transcends failure and despair, and produces art that matters when nothing matters.

Nin finds in the unconscious—her word is subconscious—the key to sensuous freedom, the key not simply to pleasure but to sensitivity as well, awareness of the fragility and beauty in the world and its creatures. But this awareness depends on self-image and self-knowledge, for Nin sees the outer world as a projection of the inner. Accordingly, one has to examine one's unconscious before one can live comfortably with the function and fruit of sensibility: sensation and sense. Once her characters come to terms with this, their behavior changes, for their integrity nurtures care that enfolds others into the self and helps make them whole too. Art is a sort of symbolic action, representing the fact that one's real and primary artistry is creation of oneself. This new self discloses an extension beyond observable distances.

In the unconscious, Nin maintains, all barriers between the self and others collapse; all are one in spirit. In affinity with Freudian analysis, she probes relentlessly the labyrinthine convolutions of the human mind, the world of the dream, of desire. Only from such a quest, she suggests, can one achieve continuity and wholeness by discovering the language of symbols which we all share and must all acknowledge. Nin's writing is sensuous, but she shows that the senses mean little until they are made to correspond with psychic wholeness and human responsibility. For one senses not so much the outer world itself but one's relationship to it. Thus, her characters fail in their attempts to live voluptuously, for not until they struggle through psychologi- cal turmoil to internal serenity do they finally live fully and confidently in the actual world of the senses. In that they exist in and beyond themselves at once, they inhabit a realm of being which imagination realizes in art and makes palpable through the interpenetration of art with its audience. The evolution of character is most apparent in *Seduction of the Minotaur,* the last book of Nin's continuous novel, *Cities of the Interior,* and in the natural transition from that book to her final novel, *Collages.* Indeed, the frustra- tions of the protagonists in Nin's earlier works find resolution only in Renate, the self- and other-sustaining heroine of *Collages.*

For Nin the senses seem to be a means of contact first with the self, then with others. For Nabokov, however, they seem to be a means of contact first with the world, then with the universe. The self, perceived as a conundrum by Nin, is taken as a given by Nabokov. Each sees life as the working out of a problem, but while Nin's problem is self-discovery through art (the thread that leads one through the maze of self), Nabokov's is discovery of the secrets of nature and of art (which mirror each other like the two sides in a chess game). For Nabokov the outer world, like art, has an integrity the artist respects even while inventing his own universe. For Nin, on the other hand, the inner world is the sole reality and the architect of the outer world.

This distinction presumes two different approaches to sensuous experience. Nin ingests that experience in the dark unconscious, the primal nature, the animal dimension. Her intellectual sympathies lie with the psychologists who distinguish between the conscious and unconscious parts of the brain and who hold that the unconscious controls the conscious. But Nabokov rejects such compartmentation, rejects particularly the primacy of the hypothetical "dark" or "animal" nature. While some of his characters do seem slaves to the unconscious, Nabokov warns readers against psychoanalytical interpretations. In fact, those of his characters who are lost in their subjective worlds—Herman Karlovich in *Despair*, Humbert Humbert in *Lolita*, Charles Kinbote in *Pale Fire*—are in some sense failures. From them, though allowing us to admire their desperate inventiveness, Nabokov establishes aesthetic distance. Distance is maintained in that the character does not grow but degenerates in the course of the novel, while the reader gains a broader vision. (Humbert, of course, finally achieves understanding, but too late.) On the other hand, those characters—like Cincinnatus C. in *Invitation to a Beheading*, Fyodor Gudunov-Cherdyntsev in *The Gift*, and Van Veen in *Ada*—who mature in the course of their novels seem able to integrate sensation, emotion, and consciousness through a growing awareness mirrored by the reader's.

For his failed protagonists the senses are an obstacle to consciousness, but for the artist-heroes, as for himself in his autobiography, the senses are the source of consciousness, the body the miraculous instrument through which spiritual mystery makes itself felt on earth. There is no distinction between nature and this mystery, the appearance and its essence, nor between man's body and his mind—except for the body's dread mortality which Nabokov does try to resolve through art. In recording and externalizing the network of sensing and feeling, art does in a sense make the body live on, its sensations forever accessible through the eternal nerves of art.

For Nabokov, then, art is a means of transcendence and, like the visible world, the locus of transcendent consciousness as well. For all his poise, his arrogance, Nabokov's view of man in relation to the world is unpretentious. The marvelous powers of sensation and thought, he suggests, result not from man's will but from the beneficence of nature to which man must be receptive. The senses, in harmony with consciousness, put man in touch with what lies beyond them—the metasensual—and cast light on those two "eternities of darkness" surrounding man's life. To cultivate through the conscious mind one's sensuous perceptions of the external world is an artistic endeavor, for not only do the senses provide abundant materials for art, but also the process of artistic creation mimes that of perception.

Nabokov portrays the senses as the origin of radiant consciousness which not only englobes man's life but extends beyond him in all directions into a cosmos. Radiance, perceived in love and registered by art, enables man to sanctify his mortal existence. Sensation represents the center and source and confirmation of infinitely extending radii leading from the perceiving self in the perceived object as far as imagination can project. Nabokov's open-ended structures metaphorically illustrate this principle, extension, even as the experiences of his characters, never quite consummated, require the reader's open-minded participation in the creative process—demand endless pursuit and anticipation, not gratification. Gratification closes, negates the present, which as a stage of the process, becoming, cannot end. Art, like life in Nabokov's view, demands a comic vision.

Nabokov's last Russian novel, *The Gift*, expresses this comic vision fully. Its characters live out their human foibles, learn to laugh at themselves and to grow in the process. The book closes, like classical comedy, in union and hope. In this novel Nabokov most poignantly portrays the mutual nurturing of art and love toward supreme consciousness, and, like many of Nabokov's other novels, *The Gift* involves the reader intensely in its creation and completion. If Nin finds human unity in the subliminal realm, Nabokov finds it in the sublime: the mirroring worlds of nature and art where the mind, primed by acuity of the senses, finds, like Cincinnatus at the end of *Invitation to a Beheading,* its kindred spirits.

But in that unknown region beyond the senses, as Samuel Beckett shows, rather than exuberance or radiance there may lie only uncertainty, doubt, despair. Nin and Nabokov, to be sure, are familiar with doubt, but they assert the possibility of overcoming it or of submerging or subsuming it under the faith of love and art. Beckett does not. His characters look for truth within themselves, like Nin's, or without, like some of Nabokov's, only to find that the subliminal and the sublime cancel each other out. If the elusive "I" offers no certainty, neither does the phenomenal world of the senses, which is constantly undermined by one's shifting perception and unreliable memory. All man can do is to go on, acknowledging both his existence and his insignificance, as Beckett seems to be doing in his recent collection of fiction, *Fizzles.* The word "fizzle," one meaning of which is "to break wind," is an appropriate metasensual metaphor illustrating the liberation of the containing mind, contained within the body. Perhaps through this liberation, both acknowledging the body and getting outside it, man can see himself honestly and then decide what, if anything, to do. Beckett, who offers no solutions, chooses only to incarnate the situation.

All three writers exemplify that modernist will to involve a reader eroti-
cally in the text, but Beckett's work, with its heavy demands on the reader,
does so most intently. The dramatic and alogical nature of his writing gives it
the force of physical presence which the reader cannot elude, must incorporate and later try to expel, as interpretation. The relationship of a reader to a
Beckett text is at least potentially more dynamic than it is to a Nin or a
Nabokov work, for the narrating consciousness of the latter pair is more
intrusive and offers more guidance. Beckett leaves the reader on his own.
And in doing so he creates in the reader a greater need for understanding, an
addiction the reader can satisfy only by ever more intimate connection with
the text. Nin's and Nabokov's writings may feed the soul or develop the
reader's creative imagination, but Beckett's make the reader invent the
soul—out of the very void the artist forces the audience to confront.

Admittedly, an inequality of stature separates the three writers chosen to
illustrate these themes. Nabokov's and Beckett's fiction is ranked among the
best by contemporary standards, whereas Nin is appreciated more for her
diary than for her novels. But Nin allows us to examine one additional
consideration, the extent to which the artist's vision changes her own
life—the extent, that is, to which she becomes her work and is her own
reader: a completely self-contained aesthetic unity. Unlike Nabokov and
Beckett, who continued into their seventies to produce art but whose later art
seems increasingly forced, Nin stopped writing at the point where her art and
her life became one. Her last novel was published in 1964, and in the years
before her death in 1977 she even quit writing in her diary. Instead she
devoted her time to answering her flood of mail so as to make the relationship between herself and her readers more directly intimate. In this respect
she is like Renate, the heroine of *Collages,* who reaches a self-transcendence
in which the lives of all about her are her own. Her literature of bread, as one
critic calls it, has fed her own soul. As Jean-Pierre Richard writes in
Litterature et Sensation, ''Pourquoi même écrire si ce n'est, comme disait
Rimbaud, pour changer la vie, pour découvrir un monde ou nous soyons
vraiment au monde?'' Nin, in fact, found her being in art. On her own scale
of being, of care and compassion, she herself becomes the affirmation, the
analogue, of a spiritual reality beyond

CHAPTER TWO

SAMUEL BECKETT

Confronting the nether world of his own imagining, a world he can never surely know, Beckett, for all his austere landscapes and physically desensitized characters—the most incensed of modernist writers—in his terse texts holds all ramifications of sense perception in embryo. Whereas Nin's and Nabokov's prose styles are fecund with sensuous imagery, Beckett's is parched. Nin attempts to encapsulate the quintessential; Nabokov, to encompass the absolute. But Beckett, who writes from a different perspective, one that both encapsulates and encloses, not only fails to transcend but, too, aims to subvert. Beckett x-rays his subjects to show their bare bones, the hollow skull where the voice echoes, man reduced to the universal abstraction he has made of himself ever since he first said "I." Like the Unnamable, man has no character in the world, but the world too lacks identity. Beckett's environments, whether human and natural like the country lane and tree in *Waiting for Godot* or mechanical like the cylinder in *The Lost Ones,* are severe and stark—the infinite no man's land which cannot nourish man yet on which he abides.

But in divesting his art of person and landscape Beckett is not himself ascetic nor is his imagination sterile. No conscious self-denial is involved in either the peregrinations or fixity of his characters, all of whom are concerned with satisfying the desires of their bodies (or however much of their bodies remains to them). Beckett's creatures are, as Nabokov's Ada describes herself, "horribly physical." But Beckett does not show the body as the source of voluptuous pleasures and consciousness as Nin and Nabokov do. He portrays the body as the mind's curse, from which such a one as Murphy strives to get free to achieve true but impossible ecstasy in the mind, which offers "such pleasure that pleasure was not the word " But equally strong is the conflicting desire of Murphy's body for Celia. The senses degrade Beckett's man, impede his mind, cause him pain, make him ridiculous—but also give him pleasure—and are above all inescapable.

Adopting this attitude toward the senses, Beckett devises a technique that enables him to acknowledge the senses yet to abstract them. He reports the numerous physical sufferings his characters endure but makes the characters strangely unmoved by their own pain or mutilation. In this vein, for example, the detached narrator of *How It Is* records his "table of basic stimuli one sing nails in armpit two speak blade in arse three stop thumb on skull four louder pestle on kidney." Obligatorily, without rancor, he torments his victim Pim while receiving the blows of his tormentor Bom, simply because "it's mathematical it's our justice"—that's how it is. This attitude diminishes feeling to a mere fact of life, devoid of any intrinsic value or interest. It is the exigency of our strange, physical-mental, emotionalspiritual life, which subsumes, contains, and encompasses but neither supersedes nor surmounts the senses that most interests Beckett: obligation, necessity, going on.

Another main interest of Beckett's art is its concern with what comes after sense experience—in this case, memory, the recorder of experience and would-be maker of meanings. Unfortunately for man's peace of mind, the senses do leave impressions that can later be falsified by memory as man seeks futilely to repeat or recover a sensuous experience or discover its significance—a significance which the aged speaker of *That Time,* for example, mistakenly believes to lie in the experience but which is actually allied with its loss. Only loss gives value to man's experience. The imminent collapse of the present is his only safeguard against eternal boredom. Yet man is rarely in the present; he is elsewhere. "We take as little cognisance of one [experience] as of the other, unless, vaguely, after the event," Beckett writes in his critical work *Proust.* And the Unnamable sighs, "that would be a blessed place to be, where you are." For Beckett seems to portray the human condition as always a little too late, consciousness as one step behind the elusive event itself. Man perceives his own preconceptions; it is habit, not happening, that he recognizes. And thus there is a pronounced sense of loss and lost opportunity, especially in many of Beckett's later works, a straining after what was, what might have been, what can never be again. In *Krapp's Last Tape,* then, the moment of contact, of pure experience, is adulterated as it is replayed over and over in memory; the longer the reel of words goes on, the less real it becomes. Although the lyrical intensity of such experience may seem to redeem the sense of loss, of sense lost, it fails to do so, for the difficulty of truly perceiving beauty and pleasure and the fleetingness of perception make even pleasure painful. And once again the senses confirm predicament, man's humiliation. As Beckett remarks in his dialogue on the painter Bram van Velde, "There is more than a difference of degree between being short, short of the world, short of self, and being without these esteemed commodities. The one is a predicament, the other not." Compounding the humiliation is the fact that man knows the difference, knows that he is short, yet can do nothing about it.

Like Nabokov, Beckett makes transposition a critical principle in his art. Unlike Nabokov, however, Beckett transposes sensuous experience to another order: physical suffering becomes a metaphor for spiritual suffering. Although the body refuses to flinch at its torments, the mind reacts with a vengeance. It is the mind that rebels against the squeeze of cruelty, the stab of injustice, the strain of waiting—not with a simple cry of pain but with a wail of words that rises to a crescendo of frustration because of a failure to find the combination that would somehow put everything right by making sense. Just as the body goes on, condemned by its birth, so the mind goes on, condemned to inhabit a body, against all its yearnings and all its will, eternally confused but continuing to think, doomed to indecision, immobility, uncertainty. Whereas Nin and Nabokov are convinced of the validity and glory of sense experience, Beckett seems to state that the senses alone serve man's needs, yet fail, finally, to make sense of his life. Nevertheless, Beckett finds the senses useful as metaphor to help him fulfill his obligation—"the obligation to express"—even though the metaphor, like all art and like the body itself, will falter and fail. The body, housing dually the deceitful senses and disputatious brain, decaying even as it lives out its obligatory life, is the perfect metaphor for Beckett's view of man. Physical man is the emblem of his metaphysical condition.

Indeed, beyond the metaphors within them, Beckett's works in their entirety may be viewed as metaphors—metaphors for the human condition. Because nothing happens in them, his works register in the reader's consciousness more as images than as tales. Like images, they are inexplicable, resist analysis, appeal directly to the senses. Their impact is immediate. They are presences presented as part of our present experience. Many critics have indicated that Beckett's is an art of situation, not of action. It is their situational quality, of nothing happening everywhere all the time, that presents images, not texts, that makes their totality an instantaneous rather than a linear impression. For situation is the compression of action—its all and its essence—a top spinning so fast it seems to be still. It includes both the single and the multiple, both, as the dictionary puts it, "position" and "relative combination of circumstances of a moment." Situation is not static but accommodates both stillness and motion.

The situational nature of Beckett's art, of course, is apparent in his plays, which are occupied with remembering or waiting—or with even less than that, with presence alone, as is the recent television play *Ghost Trio*. But the fiction too is a fiction of situation: motion described tends to be circular or even false, mere fabrication on the part of one who may well not have moved at all. (At the end of his history "The Expelled" admits it was just a story, no different from any other; and at the end of *Molloy* the narrator casts doubt on everything he has said of his fabulous quest and his identity.) If something happens in a Beckett work, it might as well not have happened, for nothing is resolved. (Pozzo and Lucky arrive and leave in *Godot,* only to arrive and leave again, remembering nothing.) If anything significant changes, it is at a rate as slow as that recorded in *The Lost Ones,* "a great heap of sand sheltered from the wind lessened by three grains every second year and every following increased by two." Cosmic change, in other words, is outside man's ken. He may be able to invent a sensible metaphor for it, but he cannot understand it. And life, despite various physical mutations and mutilations, metaphysically mirrors that apparent universal monotony. There is nothing to do, nothing to be done, only the necessity to be.

Those few actions occurring in Beckett are merely habits—or become habits: Murphy's search for a job, Watt's routines for Mr. Knott, Didi and Gogo's time-killing banter, the mutual torment in *How It Is,* even the act of writing itself. Since "habit is a great deadener," as Beckett writes in *Waiting for Godot,* action-cum-habit is antithetical to life. And yet "Life is habit," he asserts in *Proust.* Ergo, life is a great deadener—an indisputable syllogism underlying Beckett's art and elucidating why he does not concern himself with conventional plot or dramatic conflict, for such linear development toward synthesis or dénouement betrays life and therefore the art that is life's correlative. There is only this fact to deal with: life is a great deadener. It is nothing so violent as "life kills" nor so pathetic as "we are destroyed by life." No, only the statement of the condition, the substantive verb, can express man's state. Since neither how nor when nor why life is a great deadener has any relevance, action and reaction are superfluous, just so much running to end up in the same place. All the artist can do is to show the situation—universal, unadorned—an x-ray vision revealing the skeleton and the fatal disease of life.

Art as situation has important implications for Beckett's vision. For in presenting a situation rather than interpolating it into a tale (which would in turn be interpreted and further removed from its essence and origin), Beckett offers an art that is experience itself, that stuns by its immediacy, confuses by its resistance to formulation. Like life, it answers none of our questions, contradicts us just when we think we have figured it out, yet demands total and continuing involvement. Indeed, his art takes the form of our questions: What's going on here? Who am I? In *Samuel Beckett's Dramatic Language* James Eliopulos writes: "The real area of experience with which Beckett deals is a place where reason does not operate, a province of the emotions not to be entered by intellectual analysis, but by direct sensuous response.'' Although the audience is conscious (and made conscious) that it is watching a play or reading a story, Beckett does not manipulate audience response to the same ends as traditional literature does. That is, rather than leading us toward a resolution, Beckett keeps us in a quandary. Robert Bendetti's essay ''Metanaturalism'' includes Beckett among modern dramatists who ''deal with the human condition presentationally rather than representationally.'' Instead of subjective selectivity as shown in representational art, presentational art aims for objectivity, a slice of reality from which no feature is omitted (or, in Beckett's case, from which so much is omitted that what remains is intrinsic to everything). Bendetti goes on: ''As one director calls them, these plays are 'testimony.' They are a literal demonstration of human fact because their form has merged with the form of human social interaction. They . . .lead us to an automatic participation in their life-view regardless of our comprehension or intellectual grasp.''

Although written specifically about Beckett's plays, these words address equally his narratives. By undermining our expectations of fiction, Beckett's stories force us to become part of their environment, to accept it on its own terms. Indeed, Beckett has been working toward a fiction that demands the same kind of participation as drama does, a response sensuous as well as reflective. Robert Wilcher notes in his essay ''What's it meant to mean?'' that ''Many people, when watching a play, react to the movements of the figures on the stage with suppressed muscular activity. Our bodies take part in the response as well as our minds.'' Such fictions as *Imagination Dead Imagine, Ping, Lessness, The Lost Ones,* and some of the later pieces in *Fizzles* demand no less involvement than drama does. Their sharp images and compelling rhythms act directly on the senses.

This experiential nature of Beckett's art, the fact that it is presented, situates it in the present: to be grasped, it must be perceived with absolute presence of mind and body—as well as with imagination's wonder and surmise. An art that resists conceptualization and breaks all the rules, it cannot be understood when viewed through the black mourning veil of habit. Paralyzing our attention, habit is the enemy of art, and art must avert habit by aiming for that rare, lucid interval between the loss of an old habit and the development of a new one. It must, if necessary, break the old habit without precipitating the new. It must take on a form without setting up a formula if it is to reach the individual in what Beckett calls in *Proust* those ''perilous zones . . . dangerous, precarious, painful, mysterious and fertile, when for a moment the boredom of living is replaced by the suffering of being.'' Habit may be the only way of coping with intolerable reality, but it is always attended by boredom, prejudice, preconception, which intervene between the individual and "the cruelties and enchantments of reality." If it is to awaken as well as to enchant, art must disorient and threaten its audience in the chance that it may capture a flash of real perception, total consciousness, which will illuminate both the beauty and the threat of mystery. Containment of these contraries without resolution involves exquisite pain, nerves quickened for imminent exaltation or immolation. But as Beckett indicates in *Proust,* suffering "opens a window on the real and is the main condition of the artistic experience"—that is, the main condition not only for the artist but for his subject matter and audience too. But because consciousness is always "organised to avert the disaster, to create the new habit that will empty the mystery of its threat—and also of its beauty," true and total perception cannot be sustained, and thus it must be of the present, instantaneous and passing. For once committed to memory or anticipation, it joins the security force of habit.

Now, to be of the present—the present perceived without the distortion of habit—is to be part of an electrifying chaos which is zero and infinity at once. The present is pure energy, pure situation—the spinning top. A point in space and time, the present has no dimension, no continuity. As it has no continuity, it makes no sense. It is coming from nowhere, going nowhere; yet it is always passing, and yet again it always is. In its totality it is confusion itself, the confusion of which Beckett said, in an interview with Tom F. Driver, "It is all around us and our only chance of renovation is to open our eyes and see the mess. It is not a mess you can make sense of." Indeed, it is no wonder that habit is always organized to avert the terrifying pandemonium of real perception.

And yet to be of the present, to make us "open our eyes and see the mess," art must fight habit by adopting "a form that accommodates the mess," Beckett told Driver. An art that explains, puts order in the mess, joins the force of habit. Instead art should raise "questions that it does not attempt to answer." Both artist and audience must remain on the brink of calamity, the artist teetering between expressing the impossible and the impossibility of expression, the audience between the need to explain and the desire to accept without explanation. The artist requires a form that not merely accommodates the mess but is itself the form of the mess. Beckett's art criticism reveals his passion for paintings whose form at least fails nobly at trying to accommodate the mess of the present. He writes, for example, of Jack B. Yeats's "desperately immediate images" and his "great internal reality which incorporates into a single witness dead and living spirits, nature and void, everything that will cease and everything that will never be." In his remarks on Tal Coat, Masson, and Bram van Velde, Beckett praises the voracious image, the volatile form, the voided whole: greedy and magnanimous chaos.

Compared to literature, painting perhaps can better approximate the mess because it is more easily perceived in toto instantaneously, while the falsifying linear perception of words depends on memory and thus on habituation for sense to emerge. As Richard Coe explains in his *Samuel Beckett,* "Because words 'take time,' they are fundamentally ill-adapted to the task of defining any aspect of absolute reality, since all 'reality'—in any metaphysical sense—is in the present, that is, is instantaneous." Beckett attempts to cope with this dilemma by delineating his spare landscapes so carefully that the reader cannot help forming a sharp, immediate image of them. Another attempt, Coe says, which Beckett learned from Proust, is to invoke a kind of involuntary memory. But involuntary memory cannot be invoked; it must always take one by surprise. Thus, as all solutions fail to satisfy him, Beckett goes on to ask even more unanswerable questions, implicating himself deeper in the mess. Compounding the chaos with their own confusion, Beckett's characters become like the Unnamable, emblems of humankind imploring the implacable universe: "What am I to do, what shall I do, what should I do, in my situation, how to proceed? By aporia pure and simple? Or by affirmations and negations invalidated as uttered, or sooner or later?" Of course, the character does not choose, but does all these things (each canceling another out), thereby subjecting the reader to the constant stress of irresolution, disorder, the present, the mess.

J.D. O'Hara, writing about *Malone Dies,* defines aporia as a form of skepticism: "that skepticism arising from awareness of opposed unreconcilable views of a subject." Aporia seems an appropriate response of characters within and readers of Beckett's works—an appropriate response to the mess—for it attempts to hold on to everything without succumbing to the allure of synthesis. In a state of aporia, then, one simply goes on, making no decisions, knowing nothing, yet not ignorant. Aporia is a tightrope, tension, turmoil, terror, and to face it requires the admission of failure, the acknowledgment that all one can do is try. From aspiration to admission the fall is hard, and it makes man clownlike as well as courageous.

But this aporial tension and doubt serve well Beckett's art of the present, of presence, by charging it with an urgency that elicits a sub- or super-rational reaction—that gives art the quality of experience. It is precisely the chaos, the mess, which it tries to formalize without formulating, that makes Beckett's art transcendent in its utterly unconventional way: in order to include, he omits; in giving no details, he makes all details possible. Abstracted to the point of austerity, Beckett's art seduces through mortification, asserts the power of the senses through every cry of physical and metaphysical anguish.

Given the aporial "impossibility of statement" to which Beckett refers in *Three Dialogues,* together with the fact that "there is nothing to express, nothing with which to express, no power to express, no desire to express," why would an artist continue to write himself into dead ends as Beckett has? Quite simply, it is the persistence of going on, which has nothing to do with decision nor desire nor even insolence or stupidity but is the valueless condition in which man finds himself. For the artist, Beckett contends in the *Dialogues,* the condition is "to admit that to be an artist is to fail, as no other dare fail, that failure is his world and the shrink from it desertion, art and craft, good housekeeping, living." To go on is more than responsibility; it is necessity. And that may explain the publication in 1976 of Beckett's collection of fiction, *Fizzles,* which J. D. O'Hara reviewed as "Beckett Piece by Piece," calling these pieces mostly "abortive stories that never got off the ground." As testaments to failure, the fizzles emblemize the artist's doomed endeavors; their publication, his belief that it is important to acknowledge failure. For as Beckett asks in his poem "Cascando," "Is it not better abort than be barren?"

Fizzles, a rich resource for a comprehensive analysis of Beckett's abortive art, includes eight pieces ranging from two to nine pages in length and written between 1960 and 1975. Despite marked variations in style, structure, voice, and characterization, the fizzles are linked by theme, tone, and atmosphere—qualities that unite them with the rest of Beckett's oeuvre. Coe has said that "Purgatory is the residence of every different manifestation of Beckett's *moi,*" and the fizzles, gray and vapid, neither affirming nor denying, neither vital nor quite dead, unable to begin or to end in any way that makes a sensible pattern—are surely purgatorial. In formulations that differ from piece to piece throughout *Fizzles,* Beckett in his absolutely consistent fashion takes up the question, how to express; what to express, however, remains substantially the same in each. The rift between body and mind is at the heart of the fizzles. Each piece offers some sort of halfhearted, hopeless attempt to deal with the rift but ends up unable to explain it. Like aborted rockets, the fizzles fizzle because they fail to fulfill their own expectations and obligations, fail to reach the destination toward which they were more or less pointed, and sputter away, comically and tragically at once.

The title *Fizzles,* furthermore, refers in a final sense to Beckettian scatology, to the principle of expulsion. The most common denotation of "fizzle" is failure of the dismal and pathetic sort, as Beckett uses it in *The Unnamable:* "gleams, as at dawn, then dying, as at evening, or flaring up, they do that too, blaze up more dazzling than snow, for a second, that's short, then fizzle out." Here gleams suggest light and, in the context of the novel, eyes, hence vision and understanding, which may begin in brilliance but fade all too quickly. The fizzles, likewise, all seem to stop before achieving what they set out to do; they drop off before reaching an aesthetic climax. Like man's body, that arch-fizzler, the fizzles just peter out.

But etymology makes Beckett's choice of the word far more ingenious. Derived from the Icelandic *fysel,* fizzle means "to break wind." Indeed, as reported in his biography by Deirdre Bair, Beckett wrote to a friend that the texts were "farted out." The texts, of course, are arrangements of words, products of the mind—but each text is a fizzle: are words the farts of the mind, or are farts the words of the body? Both, one assumes, and with equal claims to truth. Indeed, that body of words, the Unnamable, even wonders if in using his voice he is expressing himself through the right orifice; if, perhaps, he is after all not a voice but a fizzle: "I wonder if I couldn't sneak out the fundament, one morning, with the French breakfast. . . . One minute in a skull and the next in a belly, strange, and the next nowhere in particular." If Beckett's language is a liberating force that removes limits from the containing mind, the mind contained in the body, then fizzling—defiance of inhibition—is the perfect metaphor for release. Both satisfying and repellent, a fizzle is a fitting metaphor for Beckett's view of art, the art which is necessary but which always fails. More important, like art, a fizzle is the product of obligation; it is something man cannot help doing to express his disturbance. Perhaps even the difficulty of reading the book is accommodated in the title, for a fizzle does nothing to speak of for anyone but the fizzler alone.

According to O'Hara, "Beckett's harsher, unofficial title [for *Fizzles]* was 'shit.' " But shit is too conclusive. Excretion, as W. H. Auden said, is the primal creative act, and Beckett's fizzles are hardly acts but attempts. Since fizzling may sometimes mean failing to shit, the fizzle better suits Beckett's aesthetics of failure as well as his attempt to express the mess, for to fizzle confirms the presence of the mess while to shit may eliminate it. Further, "shit" lacks the multifarious connotations of "fizzle," including failure. A fizzle is a quiet sound (close to the silence but not silent), sputtering or hissing (with implications of impotent anger) as well as breaking wind. And, as Ruby Cohn observes in *Samuel Beckett: The Comic Gamut,* "Wind broken is also breath stopped—the obscene death that attends us all." The connection with breath allows further associations with Beckett's works. "Breath" is the title of his thirty-second play in which, as at the end of *That Time* and in Fizzle 8, breath is the only violation of the long-sought silence.

Beckett, of course, has evoked the breaking of wind in earlier works. Molloy counts his farts because "mathematics help you to know yourself." The poem "Echo's Bones" also makes use of the image:

asylum under my tread all this day
their muffled revels as the flesh falls
breaking without fear or favour wind
the gantelope of sense and nonsense run
taken by the maggots for what they are.

As "flesh falls/breaking without fear or favour wind," so fiction is reduced to its bones and echo, a fizzle. Plot, character, setting, theme, syntax, all fade to mere sound, one indicating a sort of suffering, but also a comic sound. The fizzle is indeed cause for revelry (albeit muffled for decorum) in that it offers temporary relief from the tyranny of the flesh one has ingested.

And yet it is tyranny itself, a sign of man's imperfection, the failure of his flesh to contain what it has consumed. Appropriate to this embarrassing paradox, the fizzles too run "the gantelope of sense and nonsense." "Gantelope" implies many of Beckett's themes. First, it suggests obligation in two senses, the punishment of the gantlet and the fulfillment of a natural order. (The antelope runs because he is an antelope, just as the literary artist writes because he is an artist, cursed with the obligation to create.) Further, containing the French word for glove, *gant,* the word suggests that, like hand and glove, sense and nonsense are made for each other, indeed, have the same form which they "can't elope," can't escape. The skin—flesh—is in fact a constrictive yet protective glove for the entire body, including the mind and its dyspeptic consciousness. "Gantelope" is also reminiscent of "canteloupe," which may be compared to a skull (an image often used by Beckett) in that both encase a center hollow except for the mysterious secret of their own lives. Stretching the word's possibilities still further, we may find that even its syllables, "can-tell-ope," yield a sensible nonsense; for in seeking a way out of its charnel house, consciousness may discover the excavating power of language to tell—to create—an "ope" through which to escape. In fact, Beckett uses "ope" in Fizzle 7 to suggest some type of opening where a figure sits staring out. In a sense, language (words or a fizzle) can effect liberation through expression, as art aspires to do. But, of course, perhaps all the voice can "tell" is "ope," a syllable whose elided "h" spells all the difference between success and mere aspiration, mere wind.

The scatological meaning of "fizzle" combined with the abstract nature of the texts perfectly unites the sensual with the moral, the body with the beyond, the two compelling but contradictory demands man feels. Each of Beckett's little tales involves complex intellectual themes but also offers some representation of farting or shitting. For all their difficulty, several of the fizzles can be read as metaphors for the disturbance within man's digestive system as well as that within his brain or his soul. Yet to reduce the fizzles to excremental jokes oversimplifies them. Thus, to do justice to Beckett's tormentingly complex view of man we must consider both the physical and the metaphysical dimensions he explores in *Fizzles*.

The fizzles exemplify several variations in Beckett's narrative style—a style he has continually tried to pare free of point of view. Point of view gives the reader the eyes of the other, a mask or a veil through which he can view the fictional experience. Point of view tends to explain, thus to diminish. But Beckett's texts come very close to being pure presences, images free of mediation. Beckett has experimented with all kinds of point of view, and their inadequacy is evident in his fluctuation among types of first and third person as well as in recent endeavors to dismiss person from point of view altogether. His *Ping* and *Lessness* especially and, to a lesser extent, *Imagination Dead Imagine* and *The Lost Ones* seem to be attempts to relate fiction mathematically rather than personally. Germaine Brée in her essay "The Strange World of Beckett's 'grands articules' " observes that Beckett's later work seems "to reduce speech to an underlying pattern that is nonetheless easily grasped. From now on, with a systematic use of ellipses, he eliminates everything that the reader himself is able to supply." *Fizzles* includes examples of many of Beckett's narrative variations, from first to third person to elliptical.

Further, the fizzles illustrate Beckett's concern with mind-body dualism—a dilemma both philosophical and physical. The dualist can never find the release he seeks within mind or body: body will not give mind its freedom, and mind will not leave body to its instincts. Both matter and spirit, man can have no ease but is always beset by contradictions and qualifications in his thought, illness and discomfort in his flesh. He yearns for liberation from this distress, the relief of the fizzle. In the fictional context, the philosophical dimension of dualism is partly a function of point of view, for both dualism and point of view are aspects of the subject-object dichotomy. Conventionally, the mind is the subject, the ego and thinking agent, while the body is the object, part of the external world of matter about which the mind thinks. Thus, there should be a certain collusion between body and mind, perhaps even a friendly symbiosis. Beckett, however, shows the relationship as hostile. As wrestling may turn strangely passionate, so mind and body war against each other only to realize their intimate involvement. Beckett has symbolized the distinctness yet relatedness of body and mind in the image of the bicycle. Like two wheels, man's two faculties are separate, self-contained; man, striding and striving between them, holds them together. They get him nowhere, of course, for the Beckettian bicycle (as in *Molloy* and *Mercier and Camier*) is a handicap; inevitably broken or lost, it is just one more thing man is obliged to try to do something about before he can go on coming to an end.

In *The Long Sonata of the Dead* Michael Robinson explains in some detail Beckett's concept of dualism. Murphy, of all Beckett's heroes the most disturbed by his split personhood, conceives of his mind as "bodytight," yet is unable to exercise his mind to control his bodily distractions, especially his attraction to Celia. Robinson compares Beckett's view to that of Geulincx:

> He expounds a doctrine of a bodytight mental world around which the body performs a series of actions which the mind not only does not understand, but also need not . . . . The mind watches the body and does not describe but reports what takes place in the other sphere. Thus the Beckett hero narrates physical occurrences in terms of a series of unrelated actions which spring from no known intention of the mind.

But the fact remains that the mind does report on the body, does rely on the body as the matter for carrying out its obligation to express.

In principle, a point of view, whether third or first person, used to report on data outside the subject should be objective. As Richard Coe notes, even Beckett's first-person narrator treats himself as other: "Beckett's 'I' is a most ingenious invention. Its essential function is that of object rather than subject, a factor which permits him to take the study of the disintegration of personality beneath the impact of introspection farther than it has ever been taken before." Does this mean the narrator is objective? Decidedly not—and this problem with point of view is symptomatic of the whole subject-object malady. As much as extreme subjectivity leads to madness, derangement, disorientation, so too does extreme objectification of the self end in alienation. In neither case can the perspective be trusted. In its presentation of the object the subject has an intention, which inevitably leads to manipulation, distortion, dissimulation. For no matter how much or how little knowledge it offers, point of view can never be, can only pretend to be objective. It remains at the service of self-interest. The narrator—indeed, the author—who purports to be outside the fiction is, as Nabokov shows, an intimate part of it. "Lost in the midst of a text (not behind it, like a *deus ex machina*) there is always the other, the author," says Roland Barthes. The narration must be contrived not only to guide the story toward certain ends but to reveal or conceal the narrator or author, whichever serves his plan. George Szanto in *Narrative Consciousness* finds that in Beckett "the narrating consciousness has become the character," a view shared by the Unnamable, who says, "It's myself I hear, howling behind my dissertation." Even a report cannot escape subjectivity, for its content depends on which aspects of the objective world have sufficiently impressed the reporter. In fact, the utterance of a single word contains the contrivance of the subject who utters it, for all words are signs of perception, and perception cannot be detached from the perceiving self. Thus, every word harbors a point of view. Beckett's object-"I," Coe writes, "... relates indirectly to himself. Its evolutions are those of an abstract philosophical system, but the *angoisse* which accompanies these evolutions is Beckett's own. It is still a "third person" between writer and reader but this third person has, as it were, become transparent—yet is none the less an independent entity, none the less not-Beckett for all that."

If it is true, as Barthes says, that "in the text, in a way, I *desire* the author: I need his figure (which is neither his representation nor his projection) as he needs mine," then the author who, like Beckett, makes us conscious of himself is all the more an object of conscious desire. This may be the reason why Beckett is one of the most discussed authors in literary history. So disturbing are his works that we *desire* Beckett's presence to help us realize his ideas, to humanize their barrenness, to explain what he "really means." But as he will not explain, as again and again he presents us with confusion, we write and write—the only way we think we have of approaching him.

This involvement also strengthens the dramatic nature of the texts, makes them, like a monologue, signs of the palpable presence of consciousness. Further, this presence intrudes into the reader's situation. Szanto maintains that Beckett's work demands from the reader "a double point of view, that of seeing while being seen." The reader, in a way, violates the space of the text as he perceives it, yet the text also violates the reader's space, startles him out of security, complacency, habit. According to Szanto:

> If a reader is to understand the Beckett novel before him, he must . . .realize that as he reads he stands in the shoes of both the author and the narrator, but with Beckett there is another occasionally added dimension. The paradox of a necessity to achieve the impossible— to express when there is nothing to be said—demands that the reader, like Beckett the puppet-master of the early novels, also stand outside and watch the whole process take place, that the reader, in effect, view himself in the shoes of the narrator protagonist.

Beckett demands more than the traditional process of "identifying" with a character in fiction, for his characters do not have personalities one can assume, nor do they do things the reader is likely ever to do. If their behavior makes sense, it is as fairy tales do in the way described by Bruno Bettelheim:

> The fairy tale clearly does not refer to the outer world, although it

may begin realistically enough and have everyday features woven into it. The unrealistic nature of these tales (which narrow-minded rationalists object to) is an important device, because it makes obvious that the fairy tales' concern is not useful information about the external world, but the inner processes taking place in an individual.

(The inner processes with which Beckett concerns himself are, of course, not just psychological ones but also those expressed by a fizzle.) Like fairy tales too, these inner processes are universal, and each reader must incorporate the space of Beckett's texts, must inhabit the work that contains him, in order to understand its implications both in the literary context and in the context of the reader's life. The complications of point of view, however, not only involve the reader through their heavy demands on his presence of mind but also contribute to the absurdity, the mess, revealed by Beckett's x-rays.

Point of view, that problem of "knowing not knowing pretending," as Beckett writes in the poem "Cascando," becomes an overwhelming concern in *Fizzles*, for the narrators do not remain consistent even for the duration of any short piece. Further, they are unclear about their plans, uncommitted to their own perspective, uncertain about how to proceed. The works give the appearance of being uncontrolled, accidental, like rough drafts or notes from which "little by little . . .history takes shape." Beckett employs, with typical tension and aporia, the artifice of nonartifice, which somehow holds in line, though on the brink of insurrection, "the gantelope of sense and nonsense." Accommodation of the mess, of course, requires just such contradiction—control of an uncontrolled point of view that leads and misleads the reader through the anomalous trails of Beckett's almost absent landscapes. But this kind of confusion is integral if the works are to represent the mess and to be perceived directly as Beckettian experiences. For the fictions to be his present, the reader must be threatened by them; and he must not be lulled by old fictional habits such as an organizing point of view.

Fizzle 1 illustrates the failure of point of view to remain true to its apparent goal and object. The narrator eventually does more than involve himself in the piece; he englobes it—his mind containing that within which it is contained, the body of the text, the body of the character, the implied body of the narrator himself. The reader's double duty is to mime the narrator's consciousness as well as that of which he is conscious, all the while penetrating and encompassing the text with his own self-consciousness.

Dualism, memory, point of view, and the metaphor of body for spirit are concerns of Fizzle 1, where we again meet Murphy of Beckett's early novel

Murphy, resurrected but scarcely restored to himself. Although the original Murphy "felt himself split in two, a body and a mind," it is his mind (which even has its own chapter) that is of greatest interest in the novel. The first Murphy ties himself into a rocking chair to quiet his body so that he may retreat into the blissful life of his mind. The fizzled Murphy, however, exists almost exclusively as a body, for "the great head where he toils is all mockery." At the beginning, the third-person narrator of Fizzle 1 identifies Murphy in terms of appearance, in a way we might call objective, by describing his clothing, posture, motion, and position in the strange, dark labyrinth. With characteristic omniscience, the narrator also mentions Murphy's memories and concerns, but at first he is more interested in reporting Murphy's actions. Murphy, on his halting journey along a zigzag path hemmed by walls, bumps, bleeds, squeezes through narrows, hurts his chest and back, all the while seeing nothing. He does, however, hear sounds—that of a fall and that of "the body [his own] on its way." For whereas *Murphy* emphasizes the life of the mind, in Fizzle 1 it is the body which has a way, which gets its way, and which along the way supplies the mind with the data for a few memories, "a little past"—in short, a history which, if true to definition, should factually record the body's journey.

But we are not to learn much of that journey, for only three pages into the fizzle the narrator begins to get carried away by tale-telling and to lose contact with the source of his tale. He becomes less authoritative but more intrusive as, for example, he starts to interpret Murphy's actions and to hypothesize and comment upon others: "This is not the time to go into his wrongs," the narrator begins, thus calling attention to his plan as well as qualifying it by his deviation, speculating that Murphy should perhaps have persisted in trying "to pierce the gloom," that he might finally have succeeded, "up to a point, which would have brightened things up for him, nothing like a ray of light, from time to time, to brighten things up for one." Nor can he stop there. Rising like vapor farther and farther from the wet corridor where Murphy labors, the narrator fantasizes a time when "all is flooded with light" and "the moon may appear." He recovers himself to catch up with Murphy again, follows his progress, then ventures into his mind where, as it is all presumption on the narrator's part, he discovers not Murphy but himself.

Murphy's mind now seems hardly to be the pure contemplative faculty it was in its former state. Instead it consists primarily of memory. Murphy's memories in Fizzle 1 seem part of what Beckett calls in *Proust* voluntary memory, which contains "nothing of the past, merely a blurred and uniform projection once removed of our anxiety and opportunism—that is to say, nothing." The narrator demonstrates that, as Murphy's memories accumulate, they offer less fidelity to the "truth" of experience. For it is only the "maxima and minima" of experience that are recorded, those "occasions passing rightly or wrongly for outstanding." Thus, the shape the history assumes is a distortion of its mundane reality. The narrator consistently uses the word "shape" in conjunction with Murphy's history, and shaped it is—formed, crafted, designed—unlike formless experience. Indeed, as the history takes shape it also changes shape, new maxima and minima obliterating the old. This suggests that memory, as well as fiction, provides not so much a history of the body or of experience but of the mind, recollections of rare moments of awareness. But the mind is fragile, fickle, and relative. For example, only on "days of great recall" do the "two unforgettable" minima surface, "a sound of fall so muted by the distance, or for want of weight, or for lack of space between departure and arrival, that it was perhaps his fancy. Or again, second example, no, not a good example." These multiple mental uncertainties (days of great recall as opposed to other, presumably ordinary days of lesser recall; three hypothetical reasons for the fall's muted sound; the possibility of fancy; the selectivity toward fact in rejection of the second example) undercut the reliability of the "history" as well as the credibility of the narrator. His attempt to portray Murphy fizzles as his perceptions fall subject to doubt. Indeed, Murphy himself may not matter. It is what he represents—man's plight—to the narrator and to the reader that is important. If Murphy is a metaphor, he owes his very existence and his meaning to the narrator, and thus his history can be only what the narrator imagines. Though questionable at the literal level, the narrator's perceptions are absolute on the literary level as the source of his expression. For it is the obligation to express which survives the failure of this fizzle. If nothing else, the narrator has met that obligation even though he does not conclude it, and his promise, "more very shortly," is abortive.

The last words of Fizzle 1 suggest that artistic expression takes off from experience, articulates experience not for the sake of accuracy but for its own designs. For history imposes a form that deforms random experience. The narrator shows concern not with the literal events but with the way they can be arranged into elements and motifs which contribute to enrich experience. Unlike Beckett, he seeks a form not to accommodate the mess but to alter the mess. Unable to sustain his perception of Murphy, he lapses into authorial habit, and thus he reveals little of Murphy but much of himself. Thereby, of course, he makes us conscious of the fiction; and once conscious, we are also aware of ourselves as both part of it (in collusion with the narrator) and distinct from it. The piece leaves us in the grey area, the purgatory, between art and life—Beckett's usual environment. Because we can imagine plodding, suffering Murphy as the emblem of our metaphysical situation but can also realize that it is all a story, we become both subject and object of the fizzle. Further, in trying to interpret it we impose our own shape over it, seek our own elements and motifs in it, and further disfigure the whole thing. In our perplexity and desire to know, to interpret, we may ask, like the Unnamable, "Where now? Who now? When now?" The answer is always the same: "I, say I." Reading Beckett, we find ourselves in every word. But as we ingest the words we produce our own fizzle, indigestible meaning, an interpretation: shit. We do with the story just what the narrator of Fizzle 1 does with Murphy. That is, we are a body on its way through Beckett's tale, a foreign substance seeking explusion.

The scatological ramifications of the fizzle support this conjecture. Murphy journeying without relief where "the air is foul" may be feces "on its way" through the contortions of the intestines—squeezing through, never turning back, blindly seeking a way out, waiting to fall: "a great drop dropping at last from a great height and bursting, a solid mass that leaves its place and crashes down, lighter particles collapsing slowly." But, poor Murphy, "He himself has yet to drop." And because the narrator never gets around to finishing the tale, Murphy never does reach the "true air" he seeks. The symbolic Murphy is the shit of the narrator's mind, never expelled but fizzling on as so much foul air. Murphy's corridor, then, may also be the convolutions of the brain which shape him just as the bowels shape the feces. And we, reading the fizzle, ingest the whole mess so that it rumbles on, unrelieved, inside us.

The closely related and partly identical Fizzles 3 and 4 present another kind of narrative mess confusing the subject and object of fiction—a confusion that results from man's problematic dual nature. As in *The Unnamable,* the first-person, bodiless narrator continually asserts his distinction from the wordless body whose "little slow steps" through life or death are the matter of the tales. The "I" protects itself by refusing to take a form: "I gave up before birth, it is not possible otherwise, but birth there had to be, it was he, I was inside." But "I" does take the form of words, words that define himself as the negative of objective reality ("it was he who wailed, he who saw the light, I didn't wail, I didn't see the light") while "he" is the negative of subjective reality, of words ("he will never say I, because of me, he won't speak to anyone, no one will speak to him, he won't speak to himself"). Obviously, "he" and "I" are one and yet, like body and mind, distressingly different. There must be commerce between them, "he" giving a place for "I" to be, "I" telling "his" tale; yet the relationship is mutually regressive and exploitative. Although "he seeks a voice for me," the one he finds will suit himself instead. Similarly, "I" tries to rant "him" to death, for "it's he will die, I won't die." Indeed, the narrator, having no life of his own, will "live his death." He experiences only vicariously. "There is nothing left in his head, I'll feed it all it needs," the narrator promises, yet he can offer nothing but mental impressions—pain, absence, negation, impossibility, stray ruins, and phantoms from the past, "that he may love again, lose again." From such torment it is no wonder "he" flees yet remains confusedly haunted, and wherever he goes it is always the same, for "I'm still inside, the same."

In the second of these paired tales, the "I" tries to dismiss its "he" by telling the "tale of his death" but ends up revealing his own dependence on that other self. Reducing "him" to bones and dust, he finds himself at a dead end and slowly retreats to "his" past desires until at last he finds himself speaking as though "he" has a future. He resurrects the body because it is his sole source of information or of form; its death is impossible because unimaginable. The body provides the tale which is the only proof of the "I's" existence. And so, though "he" and "I" are always in each other's way, though both action and speech are impossible, everything continues in a state of anguished equilibrium, a balance of terrible tension which neither can endure, yet which each endures. The chain of statement and negation constituting these two fizzles completely confounds the point of view, as it does in *The Unnamable,* and leaves the reader with no reliable source of information—indeed, with no information, since everything is canceled. J. M. Coatzee says of *Lessness* what might also be said of Fizzles 3 and 4: "We are left with a fiction of net zero on our hands, or rather with the obliterated traces of a consciousness elaborating and dismissing its own inventions." Reading to reach zero, to learn nothing, creates a certain stress which the reader incorporates into his impression of the fizzles—a stress mirroring that in the works themselves. And the lack of resolution keeps the texts in a perpetual present of waiting, which will not submit to the synthetic passage of time.

But the present tense and tension of Beckett's works are illustrated in another way by Fizzles 3 and 4 as well. For the two offer images of a mental landscape, a "ruinstrewn land," whose spare lines recede in every direction toward a blank horizon. The landscape's most conspicuous characteristic, however, is not its sparse vegetation but the tension with which it is charged and which makes the solitary figure, "he," proceed in panic with "little wary steps." The action is repetitive: the figure treads ten steps or so, stops "hunched over his stick" to catch his breath, listens, goes on. There is only one infinitesimal respite from infinite sameness—"afar a bird"—an event that gives the piece its title. (Only three fizzles have titles: No. 3, "Afar a bird"; No. 7, "Still"; and No. 8, "For to end yet again.") The apparent sound (though sound is not mentioned) of the bird may be the rare intrusion of external reality, of beauty, of perception, upon hermetic, habituated consciousness, and from it "he" flees, only to find himself again in the same place at the end. The external sign seems to strike terror in this solipsistic universe where everything has reference to the self, where all perception is of the self or is self-referential. Everything with a life of its own must be devoured to become part of the self, or else it has no place. Everything that has to do with the body, with time and space, becomes merely an aspect of the mind, merely "confusion of memory and lament, of loved ones and impossible youth," with which the mind torments the body, instilling impossible desire. Besides this extravagantly romantic view, of course, there is the irreverent one. A bird, in Cockney slang, is a fart, the only sound in this confused and distressed milieu, the body, the brain, each "fed" with "all he needs"—the indigestible stuff of mind and matter.

The extreme spareness of sensuous detail and of motion in these two fizzles allows the works to register in the reader as virtually a single image. Unlike traditional fiction, for which the reader often has trouble approximating the writer's view of a complex environment, with Beckett's fiction the reader has little difficulty forming an image, for there is so little to imagine. All we need to know will be said ("fed") to us. Indeed, Beckett is often so precise about what he tells us that he imposes an authority beyond which we dare not presume (the kind of authority he exercises in directing his plays). His languages or environments are perhaps the only things to escape total doubt. They do contain some approximations (for example, in *The Lost Ones* the bodies are counted as "two hundred bodies in all round numbers"), but certainly not enough to encourage embellishment by the reader's fancy. Despite their severity, one looks to them with a certain relief from the torrent of words and doubts in a Beckett text, fixes on them as a means of realizing the abstractions of Beckett's fictional mode. In such works as Fizzle 3 and 4, as in the trilogy and *How It Is,* the reader grasps for a connection between the material world and the flow of words; and the "ruinstrewn land" with its lone hedge, the figure standing with hands on his stick, "the trunk horizontal, the legs asprawl, sagging at the knees"—these things emerge starkly from the deluge of "it was he had a life, I didn't have a life, a life not worth having, because of me, it's impossible I should have a mind and I have one," and on and on. Surrealist images like Beckett's are, as André Breton said in the *Manifestoes,* "the only guideposts of the mind," the only way of following the road through the mind as laid out by the author. The sharp visual image which Beckett evokes becomes, like the surrealist image, supreme reality, an experience that jolts the reader into perception.

It is in Fizzle 7 that Beckett's graphic imagery is most powerful. The narrative style resembles that of *Ping* and *Lessness,* which seem to strive for objectivity by replacing the personal point of view with the mathematical. The effect at first is complete detachment and disinterest—a description of the body in the most phenomenological, the most verifiable way possible: measurement and observation. Admittedly, this is not omniscient; it is objective only in relation to the narrator-observer, only within the limits of his perception.

Fizzle 7 records the observation of one small gesture, an arm being raised to hold a head as a seated figure watches a sunset, with what O'Hara calls "preternatural concern, breaking it down into split-second sequences as a moving-picture film would do." So "objective" is the point of view that not only are no personal pronouns used but the figure described is scarcely seen as a unit, just individual fragments as each is scrutinized part by part. Thus, the figure has no identity; it is really a diagram. Only after "close inspection namely detail by detail all over" does the sum of its parts "add up finally to this whole." The position and angle of each part is charted: legs, knees, trunk, skull, arms, elbows, forearms.

As space, specifically that occupied by the body, is objectified in this piece, so is time, a sequence of moments through which the body passes. During most of the fizzle the sentences are strictly sequential, each describing the next movement in the interaction between the setting sun and the observer. The prose offers a succession of present moments, each related (when verbs are used at all) in the present tense or present participle. All forms of the verb "to be" are omitted, as though the static nature of the substantive verb would betray the objective reality of time's passage. As darkness—"though of course no such thing just less light"—settles in, the seated figure begins in slow motion to lift its hand, forearm, and elbow into the air, then lowers the head to meet the hand, returns the elbow to the armrest, "and all still once more."

As the lack of substantive verbs suggests, time is motion, and the text makes an ironic comment on its title, "Still." For stillness is proved an illusion. To be still is really to be only "quite still"—that is, relatively still. In the objective or scientific world of atoms and particles and electric charges, stillness is impossible: "actually close inspection not still at all but trembling all over." Only in human consciousness can time stand still, can it be simultaneous or reversible. Human consciousness, of course, will not disappear from humanly created artifacts like words or fiction. Thus, the narrator's objectivity fizzles as he continues to observe and describe.

Once the hand has met the head, perhaps because "this movement impossible to follow let alone describe," perhaps because, besides the physical act of human motion, there is also the motivation, scientific description begins to give way to fictional technique, to imagination, and the narrator interrupts the sequence to propose a retrospective, a reconsideration of the hand waiting for the head, a flashback: "Here back a little way to that suspense before head to rescue as if hand's need the greater." "Suspense," a carefully chosen word, signifies not only the literal hanging of the hand but also the literary manipulation of the reader's expectations, in accord with the narrator's growing interest in the object of his description. And though the sequence resumes after this interlude the narrator continues to speculate, to imagine beyond what he can observe: "As if even in the dark eyes closed not enough and perhaps even more than ever necessary against that no such thing the further shelter of the hand.''

Setting (time more than place) dominates the opening of the piece, but gradually character-in-time (being-in-time) becomes the center of interest. There is something about the ritual, the isolation, the deliberate slowness, the head's rescue of the hand, the hand's shelter of the head, that will not keep the figure within the bounds of a diagram, that invests it with emotional poignancy. It fleshes out, seems human, as the narrative develops a complex emotional tone. At the end the figure is left "all quite still head in hand listening for a sound.'' The sense of waiting implicit in listening for, not to, a sound also deepens the emotional tone and enhances the theme of time. Waiting is suspenseful; it involves expectation and frustration, hope and fear, anticipation and dread and doubt—a whole range of feelings suspended in the present until the passage of time resolves them. Only human consciousness can anticipate something that is not there, so that the body that waits cannot be separated from the mind that experiences waiting. In the subjective realm attributed to human consciousness, time loses objective sequentiality; past and future submerge the present. Waiting, for example, is an attempt to suspend time until expectation is fulfilled or absolutely denied, or at least an attempt to direct consciousness of time toward that fulfillment or denial. The western window and encroaching darkness also lend an overtone of pain to the piece, for the waiting seems futile in the context of such images of imminent end.

Thus, as the objective description draws to a close with the figure becoming quite still, the narrator involves himself and the reader so subjectively in the figure that it is impossible not to imagine what is going on in the hand-sheltered head, what sound it is expecting and why; impossible also not to identify with the figure, to suffer with it. The narrator's concern for the figure deobjectifies it; sensory perception is transcended by care. The figure becomes more than the sum of its parts, more than a body; it becomes human, absorbed by and absorbing the narrator's and the reader's consciousness. And in moving toward computerization or abstraction of human motion Beckett has revealed the inescapability of human emotion. Paul Auster, reviewing *Fizzles* for *Saturday Review,* writes: "This is Beckett at his most extreme: by suppressing everything connected with thought and emotion and confining himself exclusively to an account of physical movement, he has managed to create a work that is nevertheless all mood and feeling.'' As the realists in fiction showed their sympathy for human suffering and motivation by concentrating on everyday life with its sordid details, so Beckett, in reducing the body to a skeletal metaphor, expresses compassion for humankind.

The radical and failing experiment with point of view in Fizzle 7

—dismissal of person for the sake of objectification—is also found in Fizzle 5. As in "Still," Fizzle 5 begins in a diagram and ends in human concern. By dismissing person, one should, theoretically, be able to arrive at a point of view which is thoroughly detached, a fiction which reads like a print-out from a computer fed with data from the external world and programmed to turn that data into words. Fizzle 5 opens with such objectification, but the attempt, of course, fizzles out as subjective.

The initial absence of the subjective is apparent in that "need" is said to be the only justification for knowing. Otherwise, "No interest. Not for imagining." Need, of course, presents a double possibility into which the subjective figures. Biologically, it is generally distinguished from want to differentiate between physical and psychological imperatives. A biological need belongs to the objective sphere of matter as something without which the organism cannot function, while a want belongs to the subjective sphere of consciousness and desire. But we do not generally make this distinction in speaking, where a need is as likely to be emotional as physical.

In Fizzle 5 as in The Lost Ones, which it somewhat resembles, man appears not as an individual but simply as a body—that aspect which can be discussed with some detachment, which can be quantified, measured, charted. And, just for good measure, the flesh with its incorporated nervous system and senses seems withered or dead, for the bodies are "Never seeing never hearing one another. Never touching." Fizzle 5 offers no characters (other than bodies at rest), no action, nothing, in fact, but setting, nothing but the description of phenomena as manifest in words, for "there is nothing but what is said." The words describe a black arena (of which nothing is known because it is not said) surrounded by a track of dead leaves, in turn surrounded by a ditch.

Appropriately, it is not the inner sphere, the arena, but the outer ring, the ditch, on which the narrative focuses. Only what can be measured is described. Although some prior knowledge, like stored data, is permitted to be said, there is no interpretation or speculation. The ditch is divided into lots, apparently square, which take up its width; and each lot accommodates "the average sized body" stretched diagonally, the bigger body curled up. Apart from position and size, the bodies are given no identity, nothing to do.

Of the ditch, size, color, and age are known (if only because said). It is large enough to offer "room for millions," large enough that it seems straight though it is actually a closed curve (like the earth) whose curvature is not visible to the naked eye. It is known to be a closed curve because, when scanned all along its length, there "reappears a body seen before." The lots come in two shades, bright and dark, the latter more numerous. Since "the ditch is old," something of its history can be assumed (though the narrator does not do so), for "in the beginning it was all bright." And although beyond the darkening ditch there "is nothing," there are nevertheless above the ditch columns of light, diffusions from the brilliance of the bright lots. The track, too, is known. Located a step above the arena, it is made of dead leaves, dry and "crumbling into dust." Although "on it no two ever meet," it is not said why this is so nor how it is known. Like the ditch, the track seems to be undergoing dissolution, a process whose end may be foreshadowed but, as it is uncertain, cannot be known, cannot be said.

The diagrammatic nature of character and setting, the total lack of plot, make Fizzle 5 a clear example of Beckett's situational art—an art that makes an immediate sensory impact on the reader's imagination. Once imagined, however, it necessarily becomes subjective, part of the reader's interpreting consciousness, which must process perception into a fizzle of "meaning." Similarly, while setting and character submit to objectification in Fizzle 5, point of view does not. The narrating consciousness gets involved in his description. He may speak like a computer, but he slips occasionally to reveal a human concern such as doubt or interest. For example, describing the lots, he first says they are square, then qualifies himself, "Appear square." Later his style loses some of its denotative authority and becomes connotative or poetic. He uses metaphor to depict the diffusion of light above the bright lots: "In the black air towers of pale light." He refers to nature as "beldam," a word with literary and humanistic associations. And that, of course, makes one wonder whether all his words, his entire description, might not be metaphorical, whether the quantification of objective information merely reflects the quality of subjective conception.

Determining the narrator's position may explain the nature of this piece. Clearly, he can view both the black arena and the ditch. He must be distant from the ditch for the bodies to appear six times smaller than life but not far enough to see the whole at once, for he cannot discern the curve of the ditch until the reappearing body signifies a circle either moving or along which he is moving. He would, then, have to be of the same proportions and fairly close to, even part of, the scene he describes. His likely position, in fact, is on the track between inner and outer circles (the vast middle regions of Dante's Hell), a step above the arena and, of course, even farther above the ditch's deep bed so that the bodies appear smaller than life. Such a position would also account for his knowledge that on the track "no two ever meet," an element of human interest that has nothing to do with the geometry of the place. He is part of the world of dead leaves crumbling into dust, the poetic and human world with traces of "beldam nature." If, indeed, we read the narrator as occupying this position, then the whole piece does fall into place as metaphor, as fiction, and the quantification of data and sense impressions becomes subjective, imaginative—the computer gone haywire with a sputtering fizzle.

The metaphor, to mention only its most apparent level, offers a view of human consciousness in a middle state between the darkness of the unknown, enclosed arena (the essential, inner self) and the partial brightness of the ditch (the objectively identifiable body). The ditch suggests the body's degradation, yet the "towers of pale light" evoke a certain glorification of illumination of the body. The track of dead leaves suggests the decadence and dissolution of consciousness; the fact that "on it no two ever meet" indicates man's isolation.

Although a product of subjective imagining, metaphor does, of course, aim at a more comprehensive "objectivity"—a view of reality including both subject and object, inner and outer. Metaphor unifies, identifies, incorporates mind into matter, matter into mind. The word incorporated as form, as Nelson writes, "becomes an emblem for the physical structure we inevitably carry with us. Language fills the space inhabited by human consciousness—the human body." And in *Love's Body* Brown says, "Metaphor is really metamorphosis; and the primal form of the sentence is *Tat tvam assi,* "Thou art that'; or, of bread and wine, *hoc est corpus meum,* 'this is my body,' " Extending this metaphor of metaphor, we realize that the most fundamental of all such metamorphoses is that which each animal creates daily in digesting food, transforming it into being and energy and, of course, shit. Devouring the word, then, we do indeed become it, and whatever is left, whatever we expel, is what Beckett calls a fizzle, confusion, our contribution to the mess. This devouring comes of a struggle which, like the exhausting love match between body and mind, never lets up. It is a source of tension and doubt, even fear, a frustration for both narrator and reader, who can never be sure, because of the vagaries of their own impressions, whether in the word they meet each other or their own shadows, are nourished or consume their own flesh, make love or masturbate. If, indeed, on the track of dead leaves and of poetry which is human consciousness no two ever meet, then the metaphor is one of futility, and its futility is its own negation: the metaphor consumes itself, fizzles away.

The failure of metaphor to unify, as well as the failure of Beckett's narrators to remain objective, to report what they observe without conjecturing or remembering or inventing, represents the inadequacy of the senses to satisfy man's need to know. Yet the use of sense impressions and of the body as metaphors also shows a certain failure on the part of the mind to free itself of the body and to disappear into what Murphy calls the dark of absolute freedom, the zone where there are "neither elements nor states, nothing but forms becoming and crumbling into the fragments of a new becoming, without love or hate or any intelligible principle of change." Of all Beckett's characters, only Murphy comes close to the bliss of pure mentality. But even

Murphy only comes close, and to get that far he has to fetter his material reality, tie himself into his rocking chair. The confinement of the body and even loss of parts of it in Beckett's novels and plays show the influence of Cartesian dualism, as Philip H. Solomon suggests in *The Life after Birth:*

> Using the spatiality of the body as his point of departure, spatial extension was the first attribute that Descartes assigned to the material world. But if man's essence, according to Descartes, is that he thinks, then his essential self must be aspatial, for the mind is pure spirit. . . . Consequently, the body is but the container for the mind. The space of that container can be reduced by the loss of limbs or mutilation and the self brought closer.

But the self never gets close enough to be known and some physical distraction always remains to make grotesquely comic even the most desperate outpourings of pure self-consciousness. In the play *Not I*, for instance, Beckett reduces the stage presences to a mouth, "faintly lit from close-up and below, rest of face in shadow," and a silent auditor. The mouth suggests the purely verbal nature of the conscious self, yet, as Wilcher explains, the audience perceives it quite differently:

> Because the audience has nothing else to look at, except for the tiny distractions of the Auditor's movements, it concentrates obsessively on the mouth, the lips, the teeth, the tongue. The extraordinary effect of watching this play is that the mouth seems to grow larger and larger as the performance proceeds, and one becomes aware of the amazingly expressive physical properties of the speech organs themselves.

The words go on, increasingly meaningless and distant from the self, while the insistent physical presence of the mouth seems increasingly important. Thus, even while abstracting the body Beckett makes us aware of it. The effect in his fiction is much the same. Diminishing his characters' bodies and sensations, he makes us concentrate obsessively on the remains. The single slow gesture in Fizzle 7, for instance, assumes phenomenal importance.

The narrator of Fizzle 2 also suffers a diminishment of his physical capabilities, a fate that makes him withdraw, like Murphy, into the darkness. He endures the same malady as the protagonist in Beckett's *Film*, the agony of being perceived. Hence he receives his storytelling visitor, Horn, only at night. The agony of being perceived is the insult of having the space around one's body invaded. Here the narrator is not in control of his space, his body. Nor is he in control of time, to which he refers imprecisely, unable to keep now and then straight: "These allusions to now, to before and after, and all such yet to come, that we may feel ourselves in time." But "now" has no reality for him; when he says "now" he may mean "then if you prefer." His disorientation regarding time matches his detachment from his body, which he calls "it" or "the machine." Having "trouble with the body proper" implies illness or deformity, which may explain why he can "bear everything bar being seen." He has not even looked at himself for five or six years, although he is planning to "resume that inspection, that it may be a lesson to me." Yet even in self-observation he will be detached, for it is the "lesson" that will make it worth his while.

Horn at each visit speaks for five or six minutes, first consulting his notes by torch or matches. Like "he" and "I" of Fizzles 3 and 4, Horn and the narrator seem aspects of the same self. Horn is, perhaps, the narrator's mouthpiece, his voice, or the echo of an earlier self, his memory. Once, interrupting Horn, the narrator touches on the subject of Horn's discourse, which sounds to be about the narrator's past: "Were I to ask, for example, And her gown that day?, then he switched on, thumbed through his notes, found the particular, switched off and answered, for example, The yellow." If these are the narrator's memories, he is as detached from them as from his own body. And remaining in darkness brings him no closer to his essential self, for he still needs the light provided by Horn to answer his questions about himself.

The probable identity between Horn and the narrator is also implied when the narrator asks Horn to illuminate his face. The light continues until the exact moment Horn has finished speaking, image and idea fusing for one brief spell of waning light. But the narrator does not know if this was a "prank of chance" or some cunning on the part of Horn, and the incident serves to dismiss Horn from the narrative altogether, while the narrator begins to emerge. He says, "I still see, sometimes, that waning face disclosing, more and more clearly the more it entered shadow, the one I remembered"—perhaps his own in the mirror he vaguely recalls and plans to consult again. Indeed, although the chronology is unclear, the years since the narrator has seen himself seem to coincide with the period of Horn's visits. But if it is his own face, he will not accept it as part of his essential reality, for he says, "It is in outer space, not to be confused with the other, that such images develop."

We begin, then, to learn more of the narrator's outer space, that which defines his body, as he brings us into his present. But Beckett shows the precariousness, even the impossibility, of the present; for as the narrator attempts to "elucidate" what he had thought was his "last journey" he begins to feel he "must undertake another." Caught between past and future, he is unable to realize the timelessness of the present, and his time-bound self, his body, is a burden he can no longer hide. Once he comes forth, he must take shape in more than words. But, just as his words are indecisive, his body is infirm. When memory again intrudes, this time in the narrator's voice instead of Horn's, its subject is not the romantic connotations of "her gown" but himself, his body, whose present weakness and future worthlessness result from past excess, or at least can be thus explained, rationalized: "What ruined me at bottom was athletics. With all that running and jumping when I was young, and even long after in the case of certain events, I wore out the machine before its time." Finally, his body is all his mind has to go on about. Asserting the presence of the body, he finds himself stranded between present and future, between memory and intention, at a point where nothing happens but words. The past makes it impossible for him to fulfill his plan, while the plan makes it impossible for him to realize his past; and both make it impossible for him to perceive the present. His dilemma is man's as Beckett sees it. Memory and habit, those "attributes of the Time cancer," as he says in *Proust,* keep man from experiencing "the free play of every faculty"—forbid his absolute awareness of either sensation or sensibility.

The fizzles, then, continue the same themes Beckett has gone on about all his life. Prime among them is his despair of finding any certainty or meaning beyond his frail body, his doubting mind, his fragile life. One further theme, memory, present in all the fizzles but dominating the two that remain, burdens man with yet another source of anguish, another fizzle. For memory is, in a sense, the fizzle of experience—experience twisted by wishful thinking until it must be expelled somehow. But the expression is only an embarrassing echo of the original.

Obsessively attuned by their times to consciousness and the cult of experience, modernist writers have persistently sought refuge in or refuge from that strange distortion of experience by consciousness called memory. For Faulkner's Quentin Compson, memory is a thing to be exorcised, a ghost standing sentry to keep the individual from the present. For Joyce's Leopold Bloom and Proust's Swann, on the other hand, memory is a thing to be evoked, the spirit of the past multiplying the experience of the present. For Nin and Nabokov, too, memory offers at least some possibility of transcendence, some way of absorbing time and space organically and consciously, of making it part of the self instead of an imposition. But Beckett more strongly than any other modernist writer shows memory as hell—purgatory at best—an obstacle to the blessed end, to discovery of the self, to silence. And memory tends to create habit, that organizing force that fights perception to the death. Memory instills desires without possibility of satisfaction, directs man's longing backwards and forwards and keeps him from the experience of now.

Memory links outer and inner selves, body and mind, sensation and conception, through the nervous system, which relays, as Henri Bergson writes in *Matter and Memory*, both "the affection . . .within our body" into action and "the image outside our body" into perception. Bergson continues, "And that is why the surface of our body, the common limit of this and other bodies, is given to us in the form of both sensations and of an image." Partly physiological, partly psychological, memory distills itself in consciousness "up to the point where it becomes a present, active state; in fine, up to that extreme plane of our consciousness against which our body stands out. In this virtual state pure memory consists." But for Beckett this compression of time and space within consciousness offers no possibility of freedom as it does for Bergson, whose freedom, "intimately organized" with necessity, leads to physical action, which perception spiritualizes. Rather, for Beckett memory denies freedom, chafes against the limits of the body, or erupts like indigestion of the mind. Like contaminated food, what man has been and done will not leave him alone, will not give him peace, will not let him be silent. Instead fizzling out in a confusion of repeated phrases, redundant ideas, rhetorical questions, it troubles him with the feeling that things have gone wrong or that somehow he has failed himself. In *Proust* Beckett writes: "Yesterday is not a milestone that has been passed, but a daystone on the beaten track of the years, and irremediably part of us, within us, heavy and dangerous. . . .The immediate joys and sorrows of the body are so many superfoetations."

For Beckett memory confines, contaminates; far from leading to action, it inhibits action. Note how Beckett's characters, deformed by the past, are capable of only minimal movement, if that. They may be mutilated or may reside in dustbins, and even the difficulty of choosing (as in *Murphy, Watt, Mercier and Camier, Waiting for Godot*) is simply another manifestation of the same impediment. But the impediment blocks two ways: it is not merely that memory thwarts the body by evoking insatiable desires but that in doing so it also obstructs itself. Perhaps more than the shit of experience, memory is constipation, failing to make something of life, instead remaining stuck in old habits. Limiting the body, memory limits the blissful and painful sting of perception to that which manages to pierce, through extreme acuteness, the armor of habit, and even then without its full potential force.

Memory, like habit, intervenes between the individual and reality, abridges perception by organizing it within a set of preconceptions and expectations. Compared to the present, the past, as composed by voluntary memory, is orderly, directional, meaningful; and man tries to envision a future which will meaningfully extend the past. Fizzle 6 presents a narrator caught in the triad of binds: body and mind, past and future, life and death. He is in the present yet unable to perceive it. On the one hand he looks forward to death; on the other, back on his life. No matter how urgently he tries to assert the moment ("now, now"), he disfigures it with his desire for the old self. The body loses contact with the present, and memory takes over with a wash of nostalgia: "No but now, now, simply stay still, standing before a window, one hand on the wall, the other clutching your shirt, and see the sky, a long gaze, but no, gasps and spasms, a childhood sea, other skies, another body." And yet this confusion of time and space is anything but transcendence. The narrator's posture—one hand out for support, the other clutching his shirt—suggests weakness, confinement, frustration, impossibility. The longing for past life or future death fails to release the body of its time-bound space and imposes new mental bounds that keep it from the only time and space it has, the present.

Even the emotion becomes abstract, stylized, almost melodramatic. It is not spontaneous, not inspired by the moment of perception, but considered and reconsidered, told more than felt. The narrator's reminiscence becomes, like his posture, a pose, a matter of style. His lyrical expostulation even editorializes upon itself: "Ah to love at your last and see them at theirs, the last minute loved ones, and be happy, why ah, uncalled for." The sentimentality echoes that of *Krapp's Last Tape* (another constipated vision) not only in kind but also in stylization, its self-consciousness, its distance from true desire. In that play, Wilcher writes, memory contaminates the pure sensuous experience "so that we begin to replace an experience created by words with ideas about that experience. The timeless and spaceless moment is invaded by time and space." In Fizzle 6 even the yearning for death, expressed physically in the woeful gaze upon "old earth," is abstracted into style. The body is indeed dead if its perceptions and pains are so mediated as to be experienced third hand (from the mind through words via a medium, duly edited) by the self, which is aware of being aware but not of being.

Death further connects the fizzle's spiritual meaning with its physical one. The longing for "old earth" is a longing for death and for dirt, to die and become dirt, to be consummated as shit—the completed act Beckett's characters yearn for while managing only to fizzle.

The image of the cockchafer beetle incorporated into Fizzle 6 incarnates the disparity between desire and actuality with which man is cursed. The beetle with its punning name implies physical frustration and irritation as well as their metaphysical counterpart—man's longing for death. (The narrator enviously notes the beetles' three years in the earth.) The insects also suggest the fleetingness of opportunity, for the new generation surfaces only every three years. Further, the narrator seems to envy their unfettered instinct, for once they emerge they simply "guzzle, guzzle, ten days long, a fortnight, and always the flight at nightfall.'' Unquestioning, they go where their bodies direct, certain of their needs and satisfactions, completely of the present: ''they take to wing, rise from my little oaktree and whirr away, glutted, into the shadows.'' For the narrator, on the other hand, there is only what was, what might have been, what may be. Lacking both the certainty of instinct and the possibility of an absolute, man can satisfy neither body nor mind, yet each insists on its impossible due. However, the cockchafer beetle, like man's envy, his memory, his longing for things other than as they are, is pestiferous. All are sources of frustration making man's life on earth more difficult. And again man finds himself in a situation charged with demands and expectations he is impotent to satisfy.

This nightmare-daymare dream-reality condition of life, its purgatorial, chaotic irresoluteness, is given yet another image in the eighth and last fizzle. The title, ''For to end yet again,'' displays the contradictoriness and elusiveness of meaning characteristic of Beckett's works, the equal impossibility of beginning and ending that results in going on. The importance of the piece may be gathered from its position in the book as well as from the fact that the British edition of *Fizzles,* translated from the French, is entitled *For to End Yet Again.* The piece conveys Beckett's characteristic view of the wasteland of life, the stark landscape whose impoverishment is felt most keenly by starved senses. The silence is palled with the comic horror of duality, memory, physical deprivation, and metaphysical destitution. With its barren but clearly described landscape, Fizzle 8 strongly illustrates the image-making quality of Beckett's prose, the quality that makes the text situational, present, immediate to the reader. Like Fizzles 5 and 7, it takes a radical approach to point of view and syntax. The narrator seems primarily to be giving a phenomenological view ''from above in the grey air'' like a predator in this place of impending death. But that does not mean he is outside the scene, for the grey air is very much a part of the unrelieved continuity of the ''grey cloudless sky grey sand as far as eye can see.'' Although evaporated into thin air, the narrator nevertheless permeates the text, for while speaking generally in the third person he also switches to second in a way that suggests an address to the reader as well as to the figure he describes: ''Or murmur from some dreg of life after the lifelong stand fall fall never fear no fear of your rising again.'' His syntax is even more erratic, ranging from elliptical fragments to poetic but pure sentences. Beckett seems to be seeking a prose to exteriorize a wholly private dream, a vision within the skull alone. Because it is unique, conventional language will not express it—yet since conventional language is all we have it must be tortured into the form which, while acknowledging language, deprives it of habitual meanings. Barthes writes that, in attempting to exteriorize language, ''the text can, if it wants, attack the canonical structures of the language itself,'' effecting "a new philosophic state of the language-substance" which, "outside origin and outside communication, then becomes language, and not a language, whether disconnected, mimed, mocked." This seems to be the only way this strange piece of prose can be apprehended; it must be perceived as totally new, something that old ways of reading fail to accommodate. Perhaps a metasense alone will make sense of it: a sense that contains and contradicts preconceptions, attends and attenuates the mess—a sense that is the chaos of the present, the radically new and already disintegrating experience itself.

There is even less of a "story" here than in the other fizzles. There is simply the phenomenological bare landscape, "last place of all in the dark the void," strewn with "remains" and with "sand pale as dust." Sunk "ankle deep" in this dust is "stark erect amidst his ruins the expelled." Crossing the landscape, though getting nowhere because they "relay each other often so that turn about they backward lead the way," are two white dwarfs, face to face, bearing the "dung litter of laughable memory," the waste of experience. A "bird's-eye view" scans the landscape, in which three small "changes," the falling away of fragments, occur—the ruins of action. Although this world is presented in terms of phenomena, it is no more "objective" than if it had been presented solely in terms of "I." "For to end yet again" is, in a way, *The Unnamable* without the first person, each work taking place inside the skull, each just a different way of expressing "to go on." In the fizzle Beckett attempts to give that old Unnamable voice, that "wordless thing in an empty place," that repository of "I," its place and silence at last. But it is still confined, still a voice, still "I" speaking for all that. The self remains, like the narrator, immanent.

Indeed, the entire "objectively" presented landscape is set in the "subjective" realm, the confining "box," the "sepulchral skull" which is itself the "last place of all." It includes both the containing skull and its contained matter, which coexist incongruously but inevitably within the grey wasteland conceived by the containing mind contained within the body of the text, of the narrator, of the author, of the reader. For the skull is more than the shell of the mind, more, too, than the sepulcher. It is the womb, impregnated with images, engendering new images in the reader, keeping the cycle of art going on. And in this last fizzle, above all, that "box" is the constricting anus, the channel for wastes which, once expelled, fertilize the field of art and the reader's imagination. In fulfilling his obligation to express, the artist is an accomplice in the crime of regeneration; he commits the very act his images deplore.

With his usual economy Beckett makes the all-containing, all-engendering consciousness, the skull-womb, the home of the total human environment: earth, sea, sky. But the place, of course, is also the anus-tomb housing only the remnants of former states. Earth is a desert fraught with ruins; the air offers "not a breath"; water is not water at all but an "ocean of dust" into which everything is slowly sinking. The vision evoked by Fizzle 8 resembles that of Beckett's early poem, "The Vulture":

> dragging his hunger through the sky
> of my skull shell of sky and earth
>
> stooping to the prone who must
> soon take up their life and walk
>
> mocked by a tissue that may not serve
> till hunger earth and sky be offal.

Both works portray an interior wasteland seen by a predatory bird. "Dragging," "stooping" and "prone" in the poem convey the same sense of prostration as the falls, the sinking into dust of everything in Fizzle 8. The ruins in Fizzle 8 are the offal of the poem. And each work contains an image of burden—that of life in the poem, the dung of memory in the fizzle. "Laughable memory" and "mocked by a tissue" convey a similar disgusted irony. But perhaps the most important relationship between the two works is their attitude of resignation toward something still to come, the waiting for all to be over yet the impossibility of the end. The words "soon" and "till" in the poem point toward change, but the imagery suggests that change will be merely degradation and decay. Similarly, the "changes" in Fizzle 8 are falls, with the last change, the release of the expelled, the relief all Beckett's characters have waited for. It is the ultimate act of defecation, flesh become dirt. But the irony is that, while the whole piece points toward an end, the end is never finalized; the waiting resumes, the going on goes on. For just as the "last end" never seems to come, as each apparent end engenders another "for to end yet again," so the offal of the last line of "The Vulture" is not a final state but food to satisfy the hunger of the first line.

But "The Vulture" is not the only one of Beckett's earlier works recalled by Fizzle 8. The dwarfs tramping face to face, joined by their mutual load, are another of Beckett's clownlike pairs such as Didi and Gogo, Mercier and Camier, Sam and Watt, Hamm and Clov. They are also one of his dualist machines like the bicycle, identical at both ends and going nowhere: "Bleached as one same wilderness they are so alike the eye cannot tell them apart. They carry face to face and relay each other often so that turn about they backward lead the way." Given Beckett's dualism, it is hard to resist suggesting that the two dwarfs represent body and mind—an interpretation supported by their connection in memory as well as by the fact that each, once he takes the lead, prevents the other from going his own way. Their "dung litter" of memory is both the burden and the refuse of life (like a fizzle), one more remain in this "place of remains." But the litter is also the offspring of memory, its expression, which results in a new generation of ruins "for to end yet again."

Amidst this futility stands the "little body" of "the expelled"—who shares some characteristics with the nameless narrator of Beckett's story "The Expelled." Indeed, this fizzle may be the story posited at the end of "The Expelled," when the narrator says, "I don't know why I told this story. I could just as well have told another. Perhaps some day I'll be able to tell another." There is no end to stories either; one may end but another begins, and for what? There is little difference between them: all stories are alike, and all are futile. Like the narrator in the short story, the expelled in "For to end yet again" falls to earth, watches sunrise and sunset, and has an imagination (signaled by his blue eyes). And both are witness to the fact that "memories are killing."

Fizzle 8 seems, in fact, to contain the residua or the excrement of Beckett's other writings, and this is appropriate because "for to end" one sweeps up the scraps of one's life, one's art, only to find that the dustheap has a mind of its own, flutters away, keeps one going on and cleaning up and fizzling out. The body sunk in dust reminds one of Winnie in *Happy Days*. The little body with blue eyes recalls *Lessness* and *Ping;* the sense of confinement, *The Lost Ones, Imagination Dead Imagine,* and *Endgame* (which A. Alvarez calls a "skull-like room"); the ruins, *Lessness* again. The abortive nature of the piece, as with the other fizzles, recalls "From an Abandoned Work" and the *Texts for Nothing*. The end of the *Texts* ("soon now, when all will be ended, all said, it says, it murmurs") resembles the conditional ending of Fizzle 8, with its murmur and its "last end if ever there had to be another absolutely had to be." The inconclusiveness, the voice that goes on in defiance of ending, marks all Beckett's works, most notably the trilogy. And the stark landscape, grey atmosphere, and dust are Beckett's entire artistic environment.

Because Beckett has remained true to his images throughout his career, one could try to match "For to end yet again" with bits and pieces of many of his works in an attempt to find its pattern. Unfortunately, all we could ultimately attain would be what the Expelled calls "poor juvenile solutions, explaining nothing. No need then for caution, we may reason on to our heart's content, the fog won't lift."

Besides Beckett's works, one might search through the whole range of literature, of Beckett's own reading, for echoes and clues to the images and phrases in "For to end yet again." The sailing metaphors applied ironically to the dusty quest in Fizzle 8 surely owe something to James Joyce's *Ulysses* and T. S. Eliot's "The Wasteland." The anguished inability to end recalls the "cruel immortality" of Alfred Tennyson's "Tithonus," whose narrator resembles so many Beckett characters, "a white shadow roaming like a dream." That poem also shares with Beckett images of grey shadow, ashes, decay; the intertwined themes of memory and impossible desire; longing for loot life as well as for death. The bird's eye view of Fizzle 8, as well as the remark, "Eagle the eye that shall discern him now," once the expelled has fallen into dust, recalls Dante's vision of the eagle in the *Purgatorio*—the bird that accompanies the concubine of Tithonus, the dawn. Like the dawn, in classical tradition the eagle is a symbol of renewal. To Beckett this perpetual renewal, this stubborn refusal of an end, is man's purgatory. If Beckett's "The Vulture" bears a relationship to "For to end yet again," it may also be relevant to note that John E. Grant in his essay "Imagination Dead?" suggests that "The Vulture" parodies Tennyson's "The Eagle," a poem in which the isolated bird's-eye view (as in Fizzle 8) takes in everything—earth, sea, sky—and still the eagle, for all his vision, falls. Appropriately, Tennyson's poem is also a sort of fizzle, six lines subtitled "A Fragment." Most important, linking all these and other allusions with Beckett's *Fizzles* is the fact that each gives an image to the tragicomedy of going on.

Even Beckett's allusions constitute the bare bones of reference. If one pursued them all, the spare text would thicken with possibilities and implications yet would still not be explicated. As the Unnamable expostulates, "ah will they never learn sense, there's nothing to be got, there was never anything to be got from those stories." It is virtually impossible to explicate Beckett and remain true to him, for he contradicts himself despite the fact that he always says the same thing. "Hell, I've contradicted myself, no matter," says the Unnamable. Consistency would hardly provide a proper form for the mess, which remains a mess because it will not submit to synthesis or logic, will not be expelled as a neat structure. Like Nabokov's Gradus in *Pale Fire,* we wander in anguish from mistake to mistake, the rumbling in our tortured stomachs expressing our confusion of wish and purpose, our inability to understand what we do or are supposed to do. It is not reason, not analysis, that makes one appreciate Beckett's works. Logic, allusion, and syntax take us only a little way into the confusion of his texts. After that we are left standing neck-deep in what the Unnamable calls "this dust of words." The confounding of syntax and sense, the impoverishment of the landscape, the ridiculousness or pathos of Beckett's more or less human figures may alienate the reader, but if these things are to be apprehended the reader must become sensitive to the pain that pierces the Beckett text, that emerges through the subtraction of personality from character, fruition from landscape. Even in his most obstinately hermetic texts, like Fizzle 8, the self remains: the sigh ("ah"), the "dream of a way in space,'' even the horror of hope which will not let man give up because ''who knows yet another end beneath a cloudless sky.''

In alienation and strangeness, by eliminating sensuous details and details of personality, Beckett comes closer than any other modernist writer to a universality of feeling—beyond that of any particular self. Overtly sensuous writing, like Nin's and Nabokov's, can lend itself to a self-indulgence that focuses writers and readers on sensations, drawing both further into themselves and thereby defining the self by its solipsism. But Beckett's writing, which offers little in the way of sensory stimulation, transforms the senses into a binding force within that complex whole to which our perceptions lead and abandon us. As he did with Murphy, Beckett straps our bodies to release our minds. Sensory deprivation makes us conscious of all we have and have not, of all our minds and bodies contain and fail to sustain. The very unfamiliarity of Beckett's worldly landscapes and bodily images forbids our apprehending them by means of old habits or mere common sense. We are forced to perceive them as new, as strange, as present within and without us. And we cannot accommodate them or his characters to our habitual methods of identification or interpretation. Forced to confront their threatening presence, we are compelled to give them real attention that requires us to get outside (not beside) ourselves so as to understand what we cannot imagine.

And yet it is too glib to say that this kind of understanding is a form of transcendence: Beckett will not let us exalt man so easily. Man remains stuck in the mud, dust, or shit, and no glorification of his feelings can extract him. Man has compassion for the human condition because he feels sorry for himself within it; universal suffering is self-referential. He may abstract but cannot escape his senses. Self-transcendence is a name, an appearance, like the emperor's new clothes. We do not ''renovate'' ourselves by lying but by realizing we are lying, by opening our eyes and seeing the mess. No art, no metaphor will clear things up for us. As reported by John Fletcher, Beckett once said, ''Art has nothing to do with clarity, does not dabble in the clear and does not make clear.'' Like the mess, man himself is full of contradictions. Neither good nor bad, body nor mind, man is the confused mixture of both, a compound of spirit and substance, air and matter, whose proper voice is a fizzle.

Efforts to evaluate the gains and losses inherent in this state are, like all efforts, futile. Whatever makes sense, whatever is possible, Beckett calls ''going on.'' Going on is not transcendent; it is of man's body as well as of his spirit. To go on is, of course, a sort of failure—a failure to achieve the silence, the end. Going on is the sputtering wind of the fizzle that propels us, but it is also the creative wind, spirit, the breath that in many of Beckett's works is heard beyond the words. The fizzle manifests the foul breath of life. Indeed, man's last breath is said to be the wind he breaks even after dying—a sign that death does not resolve the trauma of going on. Wind also corresponds to Beckett's circles of repetition and futility, as in Ecclesiastes 1:6: "The Wind goeth toward the South, and turneth about unto the North; it whirleth about continually, and the wind returneth again according to its circuits." And wind, of course, is a popular metaphor for verbosity—words that go on too long, that say nothing, will not be silent.

The wind of the fizzle contains man's dual nature without reconciling it, makes him both comic and pathetic at once—like Joyce's Leopold Bloom, traveler in the cave of the winds, farter and father. Spiritual man recoils from the fizzle, which reminds him that he is decaying flesh, while physical man curses the inhibitions imposed by the spirit (or at least by the spirit's diluted manifestation, civilization and custom). Breath, says Brown in *Love's Body*, is our essence, our sanctification: "Our breath is not an image of a more divine thing: it is the divine thing, the breath of life, the creator spirit which deifies us." But it is also our degradation, the violation of our wish to be still. Like the creative spirit, our breath is doomed from birth to fizzle out. It is man's irresolvable predicament that he cannot eliminate, that he is not finally relieved by what he is given to expel.

CHAPTER THREE

VLADIMIR NABOKOV

Recoiling as strongly as Beckett from the cruel irony of death, Vladimir Nabokov subdues his horror in delight and curiosity about the things death makes all the more precious—the fragile, delicate and dying moments that somehow tell us something about the mystery of life. The splendor of creation inspires him to confront and escape his human limitations. Not presuming to reduce the world beyond sense perception to words, Nabokov nevertheless strives with all his power to know and to value this world by discovering and describing its details artistically and scientifically. He perceives an ingenious mimicry, a supercharged exchange, between the artist and what he speaks of in *Pale Fire* as "that crystal land." From his perceptions he extends the known world into the unknown by inventing a new universe that he can master—his art—a universe that mimes the real even in harboring the secret of its own creation, offering endless clues but never answers. Still, the clues, threaded through the details and available to human consciousness through the senses, constitute a fabric of beauty and tenderness that makes man cherish life and therefore helps him to live it well. Nabokov's celebration of sensuous details finally pushes back the boundaries of the unknown; and the sheer energy of his perceptions, multiplied by those of his readers, expands the visible universe to the limits of the imagination. But, Nabokov reminds us, there are limits—even, as John Shade of *Pale Fire* experienced, a post mortem *tristesse,* in which "The wonder lingers and the shame remains." For the force behind this dazzling expansion is a frightening contradiction—agents of both wonder and terror, union and isolation, art and destruction—the senses, without which mirrors would be blank, and trees would fall without sound.

48

Nabokov centers his universe on the senses, the body generating the world of words that is its own affirmation and denial, the finite's tragicomic search for the infinite. Despite their mortal limitations, the senses are the source of the whirling energy that electrifies Nabokov's readers, destroys the ordinary world and reconstructs it according to a vision of its mystery. The patient, detailed elaboration of Nabokov's sensuous perceptions almost conceals their intense, generative excitement, the shock of wonder in a moment of vision, the delight of discovery, the thrill of recognition, the drive for exact expression to contain the energy, make it humanly bearable. In Nabokov's work sensing extends beyond the body, providing an antidote to the pain of transient pleasure, the sorrow of passing joy, the sadness of fleeting beauty. Sensory impressions penetrate consciousness and palpate the emotions; and the constellation of feelings—sensual and emotional—seeking utterance, reaches out in an attempt to embrace the radiance of bliss. Mortally situated in space and time, Nabokov struggles with the certainty of his past and future nonexistence by positioning himself so as to allow infinite range to his imagination of visible and invisible reality. He finds his position in art, through which he hopes for transcendence and a refuge against the degradation of time. Were it only this, of course, art would be little more than a mausoleum (and there is indeed a still-life quality to some of Nabokov's works). But art is also a dynamic force through which perception and vision are transferred mysteriously to those who commune with it. And this possibility makes art vital, makes it prodigious, endows it with independent life.

And yet, Nabokov says, even in art, in its inspiration, the artist forever stumbles over his own mortality, for the impulse subsides, leaving only the word as a crude residue of the vision it was to recreate. At most, the artist, a "lucky mortal," can glimpse immortality. Paradoxically, the glimpse comes through those vulnerable agents of his finitude, the transmitters of pain and presagers of death—the senses. Mortality, something of an obsession in Nabokov's writings, thus holds the secret of its own transcendence, making time and space (which define mortality) immaterial. The sublime emotion that Nabokov called in the Afterword to *Lolita* "aesthetic bliss" consecrates the pleasures of the senses, in which it is concentrated before its diffusion through the imagination and its sanctification in art. Affirming to the artist that he lives, the intensity of feeling and its inevitable collapse also remind him that he dies. Yet this paradox assures him of something more— something both of and beyond the senses. As the embryo holds the promise of the mature organism (and its death), so do the senses nurture the promise of spiritual fulfillment, consummation beyond the body. And art, the record of that promise, is also the promise kept—the promised land.

The promised land is not mere fantasy. An organic phenomenon, it has cells, nerves, a heart, a poet's life as its nucleus. Only a poet's pulse can animate it, and the pulse is driven by the human need for a position, a place in the universe. In *Speak, Memory*, while making a distinction of degrees between orientation and art, Nabokov explains the "positional" nature of poetry, which, as an expression of the poet's consciousness, attempts to embrace and enfold the universe. He compares the scientist, who "sees everything that happens in one point of space," to the poet, who "feels everything that happens in one point of time." In an elaborate metaphor, he connects the tap of the poet's "wandlike pencil" with a network of simultaneous events—or nonevents, trifles, as he calls them—the passing of a car, the banging of a screen door, the yawning of an old man, the tossing of a speck of sand, all happening an eternity apart yet synchronized within the space of the poet's mind. Indeed, the boundless space-time of sensuous detail is concentrated in the poet's consciousness, hence in his art. His bliss—as well as his artistic cosmos—is multiplied by each trifle he imagines and therefore feels. His consciousness (inseparable from the senses but, through imagination, surpassing them) reaches from the seated body toward the universe, which it embraces with both physical and metaphysical yearning.

As the poet is lost in thought, his pencil tap on his knee transmits the message of his imagination and his position throughout the pattern of the universe. At the same time the message flashes back to the poet's armchair and confirms his place in the pattern. The events comprising the network may seem infinitesimal, trifling, but they show Nabokov's concern for detail, for precise observation, and his artistic theme that nothing is too small to notice and to cherish. The poet's wandlike pencil magically transforms the apparently trivial into the timeless and transcendent. The events, becoming part of the pattern, form an organism—a sensuous, vital metaphor—characterized by the convergence of time and space in that "one point" both the scientist and the poet perceive. If poetry is positional, it is so because the senses, which sustain consciousness by nourishing the imagination, are also positional, making the poet an organic part of the universe he perceives.

The senses are the focus of Nabokov's memory and imagination, the position from which his perceptions extend. Sensing is simply the first stage of consciousness, the first step in artistic creation. Like art, sensing is positional, but in a more primitive way: it provides a simple determination of the relationship between subject and object. Yet as it develops into a more sophisticated perception it directs the self toward more profound relationships, beyond the self, and through those relationships perception unfolds toward art. The expansion is manifold, magnifying imagination and memory, through which it reaches toward infinity.

The concept of perception leads into a consideration of one of Nabokov's key words—pattern—for pattern recognition is the mature extension of sensing and perceiving. The child views experiences primarily as discrete; he explores each perception as a novelty. But, having accumulated experiences and stored them in memory, the adult recognizes their similarity, their repetition in time and space. While the child, in perceiving, needs to orient himself to the single experience, the adult orients himself by trying to place the experience in a larger context (or many contexts) and to see in it familiar analogues, thus making sense of the experience and explaining it to himself.

As it grows, perception makes it possible to transcend the immediate by expanding the memory, the agent of pattern recognition. Like simple sensing, pattern recognition is positional, but, of course, in a more complex fashion that must consider time. That is, the self perceives its relationship to certain phenomena over a period of time, gaining a sense of relativity which makes its position flexible and increasing its awareness of possibilities. But while time may be necessary in the initial development of pattern, the potential for multiplication inherent in pattern, as registered by memory and imagination, cancels out temporal restrictions. Retrospectively, pattern provides a design to the past, and, although Nabokov says he does not believe in the future, pattern does give a sense of direction—not linear but radiant. And there is also, perhaps, the hint that if there is a pattern, there may be a pattern maker—if not a god (or fate, an unavoidable presence in most of Nabokov's works), then at least the artist himself, who uses pattern to shape his works and invent his world. Pattern thus becomes a clue to the mystery of creation—if in art perhaps also in the universe—for art is an assertion and embodiment of pattern, employing patterns to create a whole design.

As the self comprehends more and more of the world, it discerns patterns among individuals as well, relating experiences not only to itself but also to others. One learns to understand the feelings of others, their sensations, emotions, thoughts, growing in that capacity Nabokov calls tenderness—a word he uses again and again in speaking of his highest values. Tenderness evokes empathy and directs concern toward others; it is the kind of love the artist needs—that which fecundates the imagination, increases its sensitivity, and thereby expands its possibilities beyond the limits of the mortal self, touching the sympathies of sensitive readers. Hence tenderness, uniting kindred spirits, also offers transcendence.

A writer's tenderness gently relaxes the reader's defenses, erases the boundaries of his mind and body, and establishes the sense of communion essential to art. For all his claims to singularity and his hatred of groups, Nabokov does cherish communion. At the end of *Invitation to a Beheading*, for instance, Cincinnatus walks away from his own execution, the isolation of death, toward ''that direction where, to judge by the voices, stood beings akin to him.'' Communion is both the source and the direction of art, the love which sustains it and with which it sustains the world. While the artist feels tenderness toward not only persons but also objects, places, and events, he often embodies the emotion in the character of a lover who, if all is in accord, becomes his muse. For the artist, in Nabokov's works, though his fine perceptions make him singular, is not single, not alone in the world. He has a love that helps him evolve by increasing his awareness of things beyond the self and of the threads that link them. Like art, love is positional—a sensual and emotional reaching, in defiance or despair of mortality, toward Being itself. In the concluding chapter of his auto-biography, Nabokov explains that love helps to locate one's place in the cosmos and extends itself toward the mystery which informs human life yet continues to elude understanding:

> Whenever I start thinking of my love for a person, I am in the habit of immediately drawing radii from my love—from my heart, from the tender nucleus of a personal matter—to monstrously remote points in the universe . . . . I have to make a rapid inventory of the universe, just as a man in a dream tries to condone the absurdity of his position by making sure he is dreaming.

While that toward which the lover gropes is "much vaster, much more enduring and powerful than the accumulation of matter and energy in any imaginable cosmos," nevertheless, as with art, he finds access to it only through his own personal matter and personal energy—matter marvelously uniting the sensuous with the significant, the substance with the substantive. Because it matters physically and metaphysically that he position himself (find himself, take a position), and because he is matter and has matter (the world he contacts through his senses) to work with, the artist creates, and he also loves; for love is an act of creation just as art is an act of love. Both are extensions of the imagination, stretching the self and demanding a generous, sympathetic consciousness. For the sake of communion, both require in-tensity of sensuous perception yet denial of sensual self-indulgence. Humbert Humbert in *Lolita* offers a classic example: not until he abandons his solipsistic indulgence in the pleasures of the beautiful nymphet for love of the dowdy young wife can he translate his experience and feelings into art. And love expressed through art becomes his only hope for immortality. An essential component of that immortality, hence of the love itself, is the reader who merges with the author in the rapture of the word. In its communion and externalization of the self, the relationship between artist and reader is indeed a form of love—even of erotic love. Art and love constitute more than themes in Nabokov's work; they are his approximation of the original and the ultimate, his meaning, the word which was in the beginning, and also the last word.

Love and pattern, then, characterize mature perception—perception that has grown beyond the self, beyond the immediate—and the two qualities work together to make art more than the private experience of the artist. Only through this externalization can art become part of culture, find a place in tradition. Nabokov's consciousness of the importance of literary tradition in shaping a work of art is expressed in nearly all his books. (For example, he says, the heroine of *The Gift* is Russian literature, and *Ada*, L. L. Lee writes in his *Vladimir Nabokov*, is a virtual encyclopedia of literary history.) For in acknowledging tradition each work fits into a larger pattern that both helps to shape it and broadens its meaning. The larger pattern, of course, surpasses culture—or at least goes beyond being definable by culture. For its patterns, its tenderness, make it possible to envision through it that mystery which fascinates the artist, the "in-itself" of life, the essence which, though elusive, is so pervasive it lines our every experience if only we allow our perceptions their full range and intensity. While such a mystery may be the end of art, however, it is only glimpsed through the pattern or through the intervals that make the pattern meaningful. Citing Nabokov's commentary to *Eugene Onegin,* Lee writes: "Nabokov's 'stress is not on the mystery but on the pattern'; for it is through the pattern of art that the artist discovers the mystery. To Nabokov, literature arrives at the mystery by indirection, by seeking out the patterns, by making patterns, but always human patterns." If patterns do not seem to form one recognizable whole, it is that the mystery itself is always beyond man. Patterns are pieces of the puzzle but not the puzzle itself.

Various literary elements—structure, themes, imagery—contribute to the pattern by providing unity. Nabokov's structure may be illustrated as a nucleus and its radii, also appropriate for his clustering and expanding of details into luxurious patterns of imagery. In his radiant position Nabokov defies the conventional mode in which linear time and bounded space, chronology and place, provide structure for a work of art. Nabokov's structure is more fluid and expandable because determined by memory and imagination, which unwind time and space as a spiral and thus better accommodate his vision of continuous becoming. "A colored spiral within a small ball of glass, this is how I see my own life," Nabokov writes in *Speak, Memory,* and the spiral spins within the sphere whose circumference binds but does not blind it.

Through the intermingled faculties of memory and imagination, the artist can find—or invent—a pattern. Memory, in picking up pattern, gives time texture and vitality instead of the usual volumeless, linear progression, making sense of Van Veen's statement in *Ada,* "I delight sensually in time.'' Space, too, has its own ''intimate texture'' (to which Nabokov refers in *Bend Sinister*)—not simply that of matter but that provided by the sort of depression or imprint our imaginations may leave.

If space and time are not the major supports in the structure of Nabokov's works, but auxiliary to memory and imagination, they are nevertheless important themes, threads in the pattern. Despite Van Veen's belief that he has ''given new life to Time by cutting off Siamese Space,'' the operation does not succeed. Indeed, the doctor, not the patient, dies; and Siamese Space, which never really gives up its incestuous relationship in *Ada*, conceals its perversity even less in *Transparent Things* and *Look at the Harlequins!* The key to comprehending space and time is not to analyze them out of existence but to realize that, even in their combination, finally they do not circumscribe human consciousness. They may limit man in certain ways, may make mortality painfully apparent, but they also evoke all his talents, all his best, to defy them. Fighting them to the death (his death), he consummates his being. The highest consummations—art and love— endure through a transcendent submission, a joyous, conscious reveling in the body and its timeless present, its spaceless presence.

If Nabokov's senses seek to embrace the stratosphere, they find footing in their firm contact with matters of this earth. Nabokov seems to discover sublime delight in the trillions of trifles that constitute daily life. Despite the reputed haughtiness of his public demeanor, he and many of his protagonists cherish the ordinary, the humble, among both people and things. Indeed, Nabokov said in one of his Cornell University lectures, published as *Lectures on Literature,* ''literature consists of such trifles . . .not of general ideas but of particular revelations.'' Time, which demotes abstractions to anachronisms, elevates the clearly perceived detail, inlaid in an elegant pattern, to legendary status. In his short piece ''A Guide to Berlin,'' Nabokov exalts the small delights that enrich memory and art. He writes:

> I think that here lies the sense of literary creation: to portray ordinary objects as they will be reflected in the kindly mirrors of future times; to find in the objects around us the fragrant tenderness that only posterity will discern and appreciate in the far-off times when every trifle of our plain everyday life will become exquisite and festive in its own right.

Through his finely tuned senses, which register the gray worsted mitten on the streetcar conductor's hand, the small crackling flame as two trolleys couple, and which see all this in the context of a far more complex web that composes the moment, the artist discovers his own sixth sense, a distillation and vaporization of all his senses. This metasense permits him to perceive that fragrant tenderness which, exalted by memory, defies time and space and also makes it possible for him to assure, through art, that it will be available to ''the kindly mirrors of future times.''

''Trifles'' comprise a universe of which the poet is the nucleus, the constellation of experiences and events forming the beautiful and significant patterns of art and providing imagery in the elaboration of their detail and discovery of pattern in their recurrence, convergence, or correspondence. They also give substance to memory and imagination, texture to time and space, matter to art and love. And, in and above and around this, they purvey the sense of mystery which to Nabokov characterizes the essence of art. The fragrant tenderness in ordinary objects has the very scent of this essence, perceptible through the senses sharpened by a hungry mind.

Details form patterns through the appearance of symmetry, but, as Julia Bader points out in her *Crystal Land,* that symmetry is always slightly displaced, thus ''teasing the reader into recalling the earlier scene or detail.'' The artist, concerned with precision, will, upon recollecting parts of the pattern, ponder their important distinctions. Nabokov's use of pattern, while providing design, must not be viewed superficially. It misleads the reader looking for generalities, symbols, and keys, but guides the creative reader by helping him develop exquisite perceptions, helping him discern the differences among details. Pattern is not meant to mold but to release perception by offering the security of position from which one can observe, free of inhibition, in scrupulous detail.

In turning these trifles into patterns of imagery, Nabokov tries to approximate their being, insofar as it can be discovered. Perhaps more than any other writer Nabokov draws his images and descriptions in lush and intricate detail. He makes love with the image, probes its convolutions, caresses its texture, tastes its essence, suffuses it with feeling. ''Isn't writing sensual?'' he asked an interviewer for *Time.* ''Isn't it about feeling? The spirit and the body are one. My concern is to capture everything—the pictures, the scene, the detail—exactly.'' Thus Nabokov makes the reader feel his perceptions, the organic link between the body and the world, the world and art, art and the body. With Nabokov the image does not merely convey the meaning; it is the meaning—the final, irreducible expression which contains, besides literal sense, a mystery his poem ''Fame'' wonders at: ''something else, something else, something else.'' Paradox permeates the word, whose human limitations impede expression of the indescribable, yet without which the indescribable would remain outside man's imagination.

That ''something else'' reached through art, however, does not rest statically outside man. It refracts into the thing itself, which is the word, which the word imitates and creates, which man senses and invents. In *The Bow and the Lyre* Octavio Paz tells of the sorcery in which the artist participates:

Words, sounds, colors and other materials undergo a transmutation as soon as they enter the circle of poetry. Without ceasing to be tools of meaning and communication, they turn into ''something else.'' That change . . .does not consist in an abandonment of their original nature, but in a return to it. To be ''something else'' means to be the ''same thing,'' the thing itself, that which it is really and originally.

As the thing itself it is accessible through the senses, which mediate between object and subject, actuality and abstraction, earth and art. ''The word is a bridge between man and reality,'' Paz says. Yet the bridge is an equal sign: the intimate and the ultimate are one.

Through his radiant image patterns Nabokov seems to acknowledge that identity. Focusing on a nucleus, he gives his senses free rein of the entire organism through memory and imagination, probing not only the spatial dimensions but also that of time. This fourth dimension, however, penetrated by man's free consciousness, loses its rigidity, becomes timelessness, thus transcending space as well and, again, bumping into (or passing through, or becoming) the fifth dimension, ''something else.'' Precision of perception leads us as close as we will ever get to reality, defined in an interview with the BBC as ''a kind of gradual accumulation of information; and as specialization,'' through which Nabokov immortally incarnates an image, a patch of time and space, with all its colors and sounds, textures and scents, and refines it into art through which, perhaps, both reader and artist will glimpse its mystery, its fragrant tenderness. His reach extends toward other places, other ages, other art, so that the image on the page radiates outward while implicating the reader further and further until finally the whole constellation dissolves in the azure of art.

Behind his intricate images Nabokov spies a marvelous backdrop, lovely yet undefinable, which frustrates him into writing, that he may determine his relationship to it and discover the source of his bliss. Attempting to understand this mystery, the writer reaches toward union, toward the essence of art and love. The sense of mystery is the artist's burden, that nympholepsy, as he says in *Lolita,* which compels him to achieve the unattainable and to express the inexpressible. As Lee puts it, ''If a mystery lies at the center of human existence, the ambiguities of love and of artistic creation are the only means of exploring that mystery.'' In *The Gift,* for example, Nabokov's protagonist, the young writer Fyodor Gudunov-Cherdyntsev, feels this mystery most poignantly while falling in love with his muse, Zina Mertz. He calls it ''the strangeness of life, the strangeness of its magic, as if a corner of it had been turned back and he had glimpsed its unusual lining.'' Born of an epiphany, the sense of strangeness includes more than the present yet is also the present itself, a distillation of the moment's network of details. The mystery, the essence, the experiential world is at once here and now as well as before and after. While the reach toward mystery takes the artist further from himself, simultaneously it returns him to earth, to the senses where all begins, to the intensely experienced detail, the trillions of trifles, all those fragile transparent things through which we acquire our vision.

The artist finds his happiness in the intuition of mystery, which generates the drive to express. And that feeling has a simple, sensuous source, says Fyodor in *The Gift*. It may be found in "such things as the velvetiness of the air, three emerald lime leaves that had got into the lamplight, the icy cold beer, the lunary volcanoes of mashed potato, vague voices, the stars among the ruins of clouds." The thing itself contains the feeling, which is then perceived by the mind-in-body. Particularly, the senses artistically tuned to connect air and velvet, emeralds and leaves (that is, to see them as parts of a pattern) approach the mystery which is both nucleus and circumference of the universe and of the poet's consciousness. "The shadows of my world extend beyond the skyline of the page," writes Fyodor at the end of *The Gift*. Yet were it not for the page—art giving substance to the shadow—there could be no extension, no generative source.

An artist needs a microscopic vision—that of a scientist—to scrutinize subjects and landscapes, to analyze their quirks and quiddities. Yet at the same time the artist-naturalist can never lose sight of the whole. Details, weaving through Nabokov's prose like the butterflies he loves, may remind us of those possible "links between butterflies and the central problems of nature" he posits in *Speak, Memory*. Just so, there is a macrocosmic significance in details, of which the universe is a composite and without which art is mere doggerel. In the introduction to his translation of Pushkin's *Eugene Onegin*, Nabokov states, "In art as in science there is no delight without the detail."

Like butterflies, details not only give texture within Nabokov's work but also point to the artist both in and beyond it, give clues to his presence and his meaning. These clues are all the more deceptive in being so simple. They present themselves as part of an extraordinarily complex design yet, when unraveled, bare a truth plain and unaffected: if there is anything in heaven or on earth that can be called divine, it is the miracle of perception; and if there is anything for which human beings are created it is to notice as much as they can; and if there is anything like an afterlife it must be the incarnation of memory and imagination in art. And the quality of both the artist's perceptions and those of his audience, on which art depends, is determined by how much each has encouraged his senses to receive, his consciousness to register, his memory to record. Like the crumb of Proust's madeleine, detail feeds memory and in so doing nourishes the soul.

So important is detail in Nabokov's novels that it takes precedence over plot. The pace of his novels is slow, though the prose is explosive. Each highlight in the sequence of events radiates with details like fireworks, the story sparkling with perceptions. It is perhaps for this reason that Nabokov's novels (except for *Lolita*) have not been popular as films, which generally need faster action. Werner Fassbinder's film version of *Despair* was a somewhat successful attempt to tell a story on film through details, perceivable because of the slow pace and repetition of scenes rather than through action. Bader writes that the main interest in Nabokov's novels is "in the pattern and shimmer of details." And, she continues,

> The aesthetic pleasure of contemplating a pattern of details rivals and surpasses the interest of conventional plot and character development. Instead of a continuous fictional landscape we are left with flashes of verbal wit and emotional insight whose very discontinuities underline the mysteries of human consciousness and the struggle to present this mystery. . . .Nabokov's style aims to give a sense of the world as sensual experience, as a series of impressions coalescing in patches of vivid scenes, only to dissolve in further images.

Since many of Nabokov's novels are about literary creation, their plots follow the protagonists' maturation into art. In particular, such works as *The Gift, The Real Life of Sebastian Knight, Lolita, Pale Fire,* and *Ada* explore the expansion of an artist's consciousness, its extension from the individual through some form of love toward a pattern that gives meaning to experience and shapes the work of art. While each novel contains a story, its greatest interest lies in its elaborate images and the patterns into which they are arranged. As Bobbie Ann Mason says in her *Nabokov's Garden,* which explores the moral perspective of *Ada,* "the texture of artistic perceptions . . .emerges as the most enduring facet of Nabokov's art—the delicate caressing of fine pinpoint perceptions which gain precedence over more 'profound' or 'moral' truths."

With growth of consciousness as plot, these novels evolve, appropriately, not out of action but out of perception. In fact, perception is action, for it involves participation in life and art, described in *The Gift* as the reach toward an ultimate "supersensory insight" accompanied by "inner participation." The German philosopher and physician Erwin Straus in his book *The Primary World of the Senses* details the evolution of perception through participation, and his terminology may help to elucidate the sensuous origins and artistic ends of perception. Straus describes sensing as a mode of being alive and as a category of becoming. That is, besides its spatial imperative, sensing has a temporal aspect involving orientation (like Nabokov's positioning) in relation to past and present, and direction and change as a result of that orientation. For, Straus says, "Man and animal in orienting themselves reach out beyond the present and strive for fulfillment and completion of a situation at first experienced as incomplete and partial." Thus does art outreach the finite.

If one end of art is communion, another aspect of sensing, in Straus's definition, is relevant—its sympathetic nature. The senses mediate between the self and the world, he says: "In sensing we experience ourselves in and with our world." But before it can be communicated sensing must be detached partially from the self that senses; it must be translated into words, the embodiment of knowing. "In sensing, everything is for me; it *is*, at all, only as it is for me," Straus says. "But knowing seeks the 'in itself' of things." Knowing demands distance from the self, yet also a self that knows.

Between sensing and knowing lies perception, a form of knowing that adds a visionary dimension to this cognitive composite. Perception is to sensing as insight is to sight, and this sanctification is humanly inevitable. In *The Gift* Fyodor writes that "anything which comes into the focus of human thinking is spiritualized....for those in the know, matter turns into an incorporeal play of mysterious forces." Pattern emerges through perception, Straus suggests, for "insofar as perception is sensory perception, it is a determination of sensory impressions." And since "it is of my perceptions that I can and wish to communicate," perception is the foundation of art—man's highest, or most spiritual, form of communication.

Perception is, then, active, for it grows from a multiplex participation by the perceiver—in his own sensory experiences, in the things-in-themselves which make up the world, in his insights into and arrangements of those things so that they make sense, and in the transmission of his sense of things to others. By virtue of its involvement with both self and world, its involvement with becoming and hence change—because, too, perception permits insight into the texture of time and space in a way conventional plot cannot—the principle of perception enables Nabokov to develop a radical thesis in his novels as well as in his own autobiography. Indeed, Nabokov's perceptions unfold and connect like plot. Yet because the childlike wonder of perception remains even as the maturing artist begins to ask questions, to surmise and to express, Nabokov's works remain sensuous even in their artifice; and the answers to questions they raise are found in their sensuous details. Awareness, Nabokov implies, traverses boundaries: inspired by art, it extends, expands the human domain.

Nabokov, detailing in *Speak, Memory* the growth of his own prodigious consciousness, his evolution toward art, explores that "Eden of visual and tactile sensations'' which his early impressions implanted forever in his mind. Confessing himself a synesthete, he explains his ''colored hearing,'' which his mother shared and therefore fostered. His mother encouraged his sensitiveness to visual stimulation, and a drawing teacher made him apply the gift, strengthening both perception and memory. Because of the relationship he makes between love and art, Nabokov's growth in art in *Speak, Memory* parallels his growth in love. He shows that his perceptions and his writing have been nourished by love—of his mother, of his first girlfriend, ''Tamara,'' and finally of ''you,'' the book's addressee, Nabokov's wife, to whom all his works are dedicated. Like his novels, the autobiography reaches toward the *lecteur sympathique,* who is brought into its pattern and incorporated into its rich fabric of details.

The excitement of the senses, that appreciation of detail which sensation brings to consciousness, and exaltation of love flow from Nabokov's life to his art. He endows many of his protagonists with a superior awareness, increase of which becomes the substance of the novel. *The Gift,* for example, strikingly shows Nabokov's radiant consciousness; the novel clearly portrays how perception, instilled in memory and imagination, evolves toward a sense of life's pattern. Pattern, in turn, mirrored in art, unfolds a vision of the world ''beyond the skyline of the page'' and gives clues to its mystery. And mystery, finally, is affirmed by the artist's love, his greatest mystery, which multiplies his senses by those of the lover and also deepens his understanding of the miraculous continuity of life. While *The Gift* covers only three and a half years in the life of Fyodor Gudunov-Cherdyntsev, these are the years in which his creative genius flowers: he publishes his first two books, struggles to write about his father, and plans a novel. *The Gift* also takes us into Fyodor's past through his poems about his childhood, where we see his early perceptions, the first stages of his aesthetics of detail.

The mature artist's consciousness, more generous than the child's, is rich in sympathy, compassion, love. *The Gift* is appropriately structured to represent a progression from immature self-absorption to mature awareness. The book moves from Fyodor's self-conscious poetry about his childhood to his attempt to write his father's life, then to the love poem to Zina and the biography of Chernyshevski, and finally culminates in his dream of writing the book we have just read, a work that unites all his themes—a book in which his love for Zina and Russian literature is made manifest in a tale that weaves his life into the pattern of Russian art. In *Nabokov: His Life in Art* Andrew Field says *The Gift* is ''written on the plan of a mighty river serenely picking up its already subdued tributaries and, in the process, gradually but unmistakenly expanding its shores.''

Lacking a conventional plot (very little happens during the story), *The* setting, point of view, and structure—which Nabokov treats experimentally. Not only from chapter but even within chapters, these elements appear as the false starts, hesitations, optimistic beginnings and paper-crumpling frustrations of the artist. But in the process the artist learns to sharpen his wit, enhance his perceptions, explore his world, and come to terms with his creative gift. If the process bewilders the reader at times, bewilderment may well be a deliberate effect, for it also bemuses the artist as he struggles toward synthesis, toward a vision encompassing the details of the world in a meaningful pattern. Synthesis is never absolute, for the thetic spiral suggests continuous becoming. Hence *The Gift* is open at both ends—to a beginning that looks back toward childhood and before, to Fyodor's primal nonexistence, to the end where "no obstruction for the sage exists." An artist's creativity evolves as long as he creates, shaping his work from an ever-growing store of impressions, an ever-expanding consciousness. Indeed, creativity outgrows and outlives the artist, for engendered in the minds of readers, it becomes part of the evolution of human culture and spirit.

Whereas a traditional novel invites vicarious participation in the action of the plot, *The Gift* welcomes us to share Fyodor's impressions. The novel deliberately details perception from its initial stages—sensation amplified by imagination, growing into "knowledge-amplified love"—and invites the reader to participate in the creative process itself. Anna Maria Salehar writes in "Nabokov's *Gift*" that "Nabokov structured this, his last novel in Russian, as a medium through which the reader must participate in every phase of literary production like a vicarious apprentice." Accordingly, we grow with Fyodor as does his creator Nabokov, each miming and expanding on the other's perceptions, thereby enriching the texture of time and space.

Each chapter takes Fyodor further into awareness, further along the spiral that extends his perceptions toward the other-world mysteries of art and love. The first chapter, essentially self-centered, focuses on Fyodor's poems and the flattering review he imagines written about them. The poems reveal the child's primitive perceptions, his attempt to position himself in the world of objects, in space. As observed previously, our first important awareness of Fyodor as an artist comes through that early book of poetry, a celebration of his childhood perceptions, woven through chapter 1. The book suggests the germination of his artistic concerns: his impulse toward communication, his compulsion to remember, his commemoration of sensuous details and their evocative magic. The poems celebrate a dawning consciousness which, at the child's tender age, is primarily sensuous. Through his senses the child discovers himself and his relationship with the world. Above all, for the child the senses are a source of joy, of discovery, and in sensing lies the promise of experience to be fulfilled in maturity—with the help of the senses of memory—as aesthetic bliss. In the following lines from one of the poems, the child Fyodor exults in the expansion of simple sensation into ecstasy:

> I soak
> And twirl tight the tip of my paintbrush
> In rich orange yellow;
> And, meantime, within the full goblet,
> In the radiance of its cut glass,
> What colors have blazed,
> What rapture has bloomed!

The ecstasy engenders art, lifting the experience from the private realm; yet without the primary—and wholly personal—sensation, there would have been no ecstasy, no art.

But the child discovers that his senses do more than relay sensation; they initiate knowledge, not only of what is present and actual but of what is missing or what may be. At a further stage of consciousness and of experience, the child becomes aware not only of a particular sensation but also of the possibility of its absence. He feels loss or the threat of loss as intensely as presence, and, in bewildering the senses, that emptiness prods consciousness, probes memory for validation of the original experience, and provokes wonder about its meaning. Loss has been the burden of most of Nabokov's art—loss of the motherland, of childhood, of family. Absence of something that has been profoundly present stimulates both memory (Was it real? Am I real?) and imagination (What can replace it? What am I without it?). The pain of absence, which is the pain of exile, determines a need for positioning—a need that may be resolved through perception, art, love. Eventually the artist realizes that it is not the beat of events but the interval between them—their absence—which actually has "the *feel* of the texture of Time," as Van Veen calls it, for it permits consciousness to reflect, to make connections, to perceive the pattern that envelops the interval in a kind of meaning.

Young Fyodor's senses grasped at objects for verification of his own reality; he sought in sensory impressions some continuity to carry him through the trauma of childhood losses, even the loss of a tooth which one poem commemorates. The senses, mediating between the self and the world, verify the presence of the self in the world. In their abstraction into thought, their recollection as pattern, they provide continuity, hence security. But emptiness where something once existed threatens stability, for it emblemizes the possibility of the world's being emptied of the individual himself—to him the ultimate loss. Rereading his poem, Fyodor strains his memory to the very limit in reaching toward his pre-existence, that "original source . . . that reverse nothingness.'' The horror causes him to take refuge in the immediate, the senses and the objects they perceive, with which he means to fight nothingness by transforming his feelings into art, making the tragedy of finite personal experience into the joyous comedy of union and communion forever.

But Fyodor's artistic tentacles are short in chapter 1. Unable or unwilling to reach beyond his own experience, he refuses to write the biography of Yasha Chernyshevski requested by Yasha's mother. He resists the imposed identification of himself with Yasha. Ironically, in explaining his refusal to himself Fyodor gives us Yasha's story—although, of course, the writer-narrator of the book is not identical to Fyodor the character but is the mature artist young Fyodor becomes, one who can surpass himself to write not only about Yasha's sad life but also about his own immaturity.

Fyodor's perceptions blossom, however, and in chapter 2 he begins to focus his attention and his art outside himself. He tackles his father's biography, which mingles with his mother's story. If chapter 1 involves Fyodor's position in space, chapter 2 concerns his position in time, specifically in relation to his ancestral past. The process removes him from an interior world and helps him to locate himself in history. Fyodor finds in his father's life the emergence of themes that shape his own—butterflies, a sense of beauty and of the miraculous, a love for imaginary realms. But this stage of perception differs little from the child's, from Fyodor's poems. As Nabokov told an interviewer, ''Tracing an ancestor to his lair hardly differs from a boy's search for a bird's nest or for a ball lost in the grass. The Christmas tree of one's childhood is replaced by the Family Tree.''

Chapter 3, the core of the spiral book, shows Fyodor's consciousness radiating outward, reaching toward love, which bridges the solipsistic abyss. Love for one's father and mother (as expressed in chapter 2) is a form of self-love, but Fyodor evolves beyond that toward the other, toward art. His love for literature and for Zina directs him to write; his feeling of communion compels communication, makes him part of both art and otherness. Love sharpens his senses, which are magnified or complemented by Zina's ''perfect understanding. . . .he would barely have time to notice some amusing feature of the night before she would point it out.'' Simultaneously, as the senses become keener, more precise, they plane away the veneer of reality to expose that strangeness at the base of experience.

Fyodor's sense of the mystery pervading seemingly ordinary things, ordinary lives, is the source of his creative gift: the ''tingling sensation'' of his skin, the ''wafture of bliss'' in planning to write, his father's legacy of perceiving ''the innate strangeness of human life,'' the ''expansions and contractions of the heart,'' the ''morning mist of happiness'' in thinking of Zina, and the feeling that all his thoughts and sensations are ''but the reverse side of a magnificent fabric, on the front of which there gradually formed and became alive images invisible to him.'' He feels his body bathed in this strange essence and realizes that ''the other world surrounds us always and is not at all at the end of some pilgrimage.'' Indeed, in Nabokov's universe that world about which the artist wonders and surmises is not the culmination of a continuum but is the ether of life itself, always around us to be sensed and breathed. If ''we are not going anywhere, we are sitting at home,'' as Fyodor says, then it is only perception that gives us direction, takes us out of ourselves. Thus, perception must be radiant that it may look in all directions—through the cracks in every wall of our earthly house, the space that defines the pattern of art, the intervals between the beats of time. And perception, Fyodor finds, is illumined by love. He and Zina form the single nucleus of the miracle itself, perfectly matched by ''a very painstaking fate,'' and their ''single shadow . . . made to the measure of something not quite comprehensible, but wonderful and benevolent and continuously surrounding them.'' Through Zina, Fyodor reaches ''such heights of tenderness, passion and pity as are reached by few lovers''; and that increase of feeling prepares him to become an artist, to write the biography of Nikolay Gavrilovich Chernyshevski, which establishes Fyodor's reputation, his confidence, and his place in Russian literature.

The Chernyshevski biography, chapter 4 of *The Gift*, manifests the extension of Fyodor's perceptions beyond himself. Chernyshevski stands for everything Fyodor as an artist opposes: superficial materialism, myopia, vulgarity. Yet by concerning himself with the details of the man's life rather than with his ideas Fyodor portrays Chernyshevski with tenderness, shows his human vulnerability, demolishes the myth that had grown around him, and asserts that Chernyshevski's real literary contribution was not his materialism, which influenced Lenin, but his defiance of the political establishment of his time, his insistence on his own truth. In uncovering the real Chernyshevski, Fyodor leaves a legacy of truth—truth through details—to the Russian literature he loves.

Fyodor's transcendence of his bias reveals the suffering man's real life of nearsightedness, poor diet, and bad luck and saves Chernyshevski from the limitations of his own ideology. Again, it shows a growing generosity in Fyodor, a broader consciousness, as well as a concern that art emerge through concrete details which, in their repetition, their patterns, may approach human truth. Appropriately, his biography treats not only the highlights of Chernyshevski's life but its themes, which turn the man's story into carefully crafted art. Yet even this tour de force of a biography, Fyodor realizes, is only an exercise for his best work yet to come. Chapter 5 pulls all the threads of the book together to sharpen the design we have just perceived—the book Fyodor is about to write.

As *The Gift* progresses, various patterns emerge and expand, extending the horizon of Fyodor's perceptions toward art while making sense of elements in the life that engendered art. In other words, the book positions the poet within its unfolding universe, of which he is the nucleus. If perception gives both form and substance to *The Gift,* with perception developing as the book's plot, then the arrangement of perceptions into patterns is the fruition of plot. Plot is not linear but radiant in all directions, a dispersal from the artist's center of awareness toward "unimaginable and incalculable things" as far as the artist's—and the reader's—tentacles can reach. *The Gift* is a sunburst of joy, of art and love beyond all known horizons; and the delight of discovering its intricate patterns gives the reader a share in its creative bounty.

Patterns of literary and sensuous details comprise the rich texture of *The Gift.* Russian literature, Fyodor's writing, and literary reviews are laced with linden trees, raindrops, sun and shadows, heat, butterflies, keys, and chess problems; and all converge in Fyodor's memory, his love, his art, and the pervasive bliss that blesses his gift. Themes introduced in the first chapter are synthesized in the last, but the synthesis itself is a new thesis, as the open-ended nature of the book suggests. For the themes are not resolved, the problems not solved. (On their first night alone together as the book closes, Fyodor and Zina are sublimely unaware that neither has the key to their apartment.) Instead, everything dissolves into the mist of happiness— the planned novel, the anticipated consummation of their love. But these events are merely foreshadowed at the end of the book; and "The End" is, indeed, the beginning.

The pattern of *The Gift* seems pointillist, its forms determined by texture and color rather than by rigid spatial boundaries. And the misty effect of pointillism finds analogy in the mist of happiness with which *The Gift* is suffused. Because of the way they highlight color, light and shade, substance and shadow, because they present their subjects sensuously instead of abstractly, because they stress details over general ideas, Nabokov's novels are often compared to paintings. But these paintings—these images— change as they are acted upon by memory and imagination, which assist in the evolution of the artist's gift and which clarify his vision of that crystal land beyond time and space.

In his imaginary conversation with the poet Koncheyev, Fyodor says, " 'You will understand when you are big,' those are really the wisest words I know." And it is the design of *The Gift* to lead Fyodor toward mature understanding, to make him "big." The child of the early poems (and the vain young man who writes those poems) is self-absorbed, while the artist at the end of the book absorbs and is absorbed by the world, comprehends both fulfillment and loss, surpasses himself, reaches toward kindred spirits, and together they create a universe.

In looking at one's life through art, as Fyodor does, one can make familiar what has been strange. Repetition of experience in artistic form makes a pattern that Fyodor, for want of a better term, calls fate—the agent whose machinations finally bring him and Zina together, the moves forming a complicated design apparent only in retrospect. But fate, whatever it may be, would have been powerless without other forces equally strong: Fyodor and Zina's love for each other and the art that unites them forever. If they were only at the mercy of the artist, Fyodor and Zina would be caught in the pattern, but art is a two-way mirror, and on the other side is an audience through whose minds the couple can dance an infinity of patterns. The mature artist who has written *The Gift* knows that, while his consciousness has grown enough to conceive the whole pattern, the pattern will continue to etch itself on the universe beyond his perceptions (although, perhaps, not beyond his imagination). In his envoi to *The Gift* Fyodor gives the book its wings and sends it into the world with these final words: "The shadows of my world extend beyond the skyline of the page, blue as tomorrow's morning haze—nor does this terminate the phrase."

The book's reach toward the reader is prefigured in one thread of its pattern—literary reviews—and Fyodor's maturation is shown as his attitude toward them changes. The laudatory review Fyodor dreams up in response to his book of poems in chapter 2 collapses into an April fool's joke, and the young artist is chagrined at his vanity. Later he reads reviews of one of Koncheyev's poems, anticipating that the critic may deplore it. But when the critic does pan the poem Fyodor recognizes his own malice, realizes the flattery inherent in the critic's hostility, and even feels disappointed "that no one wrote about *him* like that." However, as he becomes engrossed in his own undertaking, the Chernyshevski book, Fyodor gains a sense of belonging in the world of artists, a feeling that has nothing to do with the opinions of reviewers, and he can read favorable comments on Koncheyev with "indifference to another's fame"—a sign of his waning selfishness of spirit.

Finally, by the time his book on Chernyshevski is reviewed Fyodor has come to terms with critical appraisal. The uniformly harsh opinions (only Koncheyev praises the book) cause him no despair but a great deal of amusement. Their misinterpretations betray their authors' differences from Fyodor, their artistic inferiority. Having ignored details in favor of abstruse generalities, they have been transported by their own trains of thought far off the track of the book under scrutiny. That ideologically opposed critics each find the book disposed toward their enemies only verifies Fyodor's success:

he had written impartially, traversing "this narrow ridge between my own truth and a caricature of it," so that the biography reproduces Fyodor's multilevel thinking, in which the mind not only sees but sees that it sees, and from what perspective—the nearest possible approach to truth in art. Thus, Fyodor's authorial presence in his biography of Chernyshevski (within his book he proclaims, "The motifs of Chernyshevski's life are now obedient to me") cannot simply be passed off as the extreme self-confidence one reviewer attributes to him. More significantly, it represents a concession to the problem of point of view. That is, to conceal himself would be hypocrisy, infidelity to Chernyshevski's life as well as to Fyodor's art, and false modesty to boot. For the writer's pencil is his magic wand, without which the world of art, be it fictional or biographical, would not exist. Just as God is said to be mirrored in his creation, man, so is the artist mirrored in his literary characters. It cannot be helped. Since the artist has no means of understanding them other than his own mind, their minds assume aspects of his.

In placing himself in the work of art, Fyodor mimes his creator Nabokov, who makes his presence felt in all his writings. This presence, this concession to point of view as a problem, is one approach to the dilemma felt by many modernist writers who could no longer accept the omniscience assumed by their predecessors. Nabokov's way of handling the problem insists on the uniqueness of perception, deprives a reader of passivity, demands his involvement and personal reaction. Such intrusion marks an artist as courageous, willing to acknowledge the limitations of art, to admit that no matter how he tries he has only his own powers of intuition and cognition, stretched by perception and imagination yet limited by the materials and experiences available. Ironically, while the admission may show human limitation it does not cause the work of art to collapse but again permits expansion beyond failure, despite failure, toward the realm of human tenderness from which art is drawn and which makes art available to the reader, who in his turn furthers its reach.

The dubious reliability of point of view is a theme in several of Nabokov's novels—most conspicuously the English ones, which represent the best of his mature artistic talent. *The Real Life of Sebastian Knight,* for example, questions the reliability and relativity of point of view as the narrator, V., tries to discover the truth of his dead brother's life. But his contacts with Sebastian's acquaintances complicate his search by uncovering several versions of the truth, and the details of Sebastian's life become entangled with those of his novels. *Lolita, Pale Fire,* and *Ada,* each depicting an editor as well as an artist, again illustrate the relativity of art. For the editor's point of view tends to distort the artist's perspective. In *Transparent Things* an editor achieves the status of protagonist, Hugh Person, himself a transparent thing standing between the artist's conception and the reader's perception. Even Nabokov served such a function in translating and commenting on Pushkin, making his fellow artist more accessible, certainly, but also giving us still another view of Nabokov through Pushkin.

Ada, which, like *The Gift*, is a story of perception flowering into art, discloses in the end that form of perfidy art undergoes on publication. The novel's intrusions and omissions (editor Ronald Oranger not only inserts a few irrelevant explanations but apparently neglects to remove some of the marginal notes in Van and Ada's manuscript) add to the design certain lines which at first seem out of place. The concluding paragraphs are in fact a publisher's blurb—an absolute distortion of tone. Yet despite his rudeness of mind and art the editor is a necessary middleman between artist and reader, an extension of the artist's reach as well as a confirmation of the reader's removal from the artist's control. While still one further remove from the ''now transparent, now dimming, dimension'' where Nabokov, interviewed by Alfred Appel, said that art ideally exists, the editorial process is essential for a work to make its mark. The miracle is that art survives at all, as even a pale fire of the artist's flamboyant dream.

As *The Gift* reaches out to the reader in its closing lines, so too does *Ada*. This late novel thus completes the spiral of artistic perception that begins in the child's senses, in Van and Ada's erotic adolescent play. And the editor, an important figure in that spiral, cannot be ignored. Presumably, the editor writes the blurb with which *Ada* closes—the blurb that incites readers to buy and read the book. Despite its slick superficiality, the blurb fits the novel in a curious way: its commercial perspective acknowledges and distorts the artistic world of the book in somewhat the same way that Antiterra acknowledges and distorts Terra. There are enough congruences to make the novel recognizable in the blurb; its highlights (though grossly oversimplified) are there, as are its themes (or leitmotifs) and the riches of its sensuous texture, its ''delicacy of pictorial detail.'' Even the theme of time is given tribute, for the last words of the book, ''and much, much more,'' suggest that continuous becoming which is part of Van Veen's definition of time. Furthermore, as much as the blurb is a parody of salesmanship, it is an appeal to the reader, whose curiosity and excitement are evoked by this attempt to involve him in the novel, to make him imagine (or in this case remember) it.

In recognizing the problem of point of view and reaching toward the reader, Nabokov seems to affirm that perception comes to fulfillment when shared. In his book on Nikolai Gogol he speaks of the pride an author feels if his work can elicit a ''radiant smile of perfect satisfaction, a purr of beatitude'' in ''his readers, or more exactly some of his readers.'' Reading can be as creative as writing, as personal, as individualistic, as Nabokov argues eloquently in his *Lectures on Literature*. There is a rapture in this correspondence, this shared point of view. Point of view is the nucleus of perception—both artist's and reader's position in relation to art. The artist offers his perceptions to those readers who can reach them, yet each reader is another nucleus with his own perspective on the pattern. Given human limits, this is just the approximation of the infinite to which art aspires— infinite relativity, in which it mimes the universe. For, as L. L. Lee points out, "The artistic pattern is the pattern of the universe: a thing exists, but it is not simple; for it looks different from a different position."

In perceiving the pattern by which Nabokov has structured his works, a pattern of which he is the conscious (and self-conscious) center, we become aesthetically implicated in the design, trying to unravel the web of deceit and delight woven for us. Thus, the pattern is another way of involving the reader in the work. Julia Bader maintains that "emotional participation is achieved through the repetition of formal patterns." And, according to William Carroll in "Nabokov's Signs and Symbols," "The author's self-consciousness does not distance us . . .rather, it draws us into the web of aesthetic responsibility," so that "the relationship established between solver and composer, reader and author, is thus a bond of sharing."

If the writer's and the reader's perceptions meet in the work of art, and if the writer, like Nabokov, maintains that his ideal readers are those whose perceptions resemble his own, then he is serving both himself and his readers by showing them, like the snowflakes drifting past the windows in *Speak, Memory*, "how the trick was done and how simple it was." Nabokov has made mimicry an art form—mimicking his own life, his own works—and the reader who can partake of his art must, in a way, mimic the writer's consciousness. But the fascinating thing about mimicry, as among insects, is that it never matches perfectly; it is always as unique, as astonishing, as the original. As with the patterns of Nabokov's works, the differences are as important as the similarities, and it is in attention to details, wherein differences lie, that aesthetic perception reveals itself.

Nabokov takes pains to present readers with impressions whose precision and refinement of detail make them reflect as accurately as possible the meeting of the writer's mind with the world he perceives—exuberantly mimetic and, simultaneously, inimitable. Confronted with the boundaries of the sensuous world, the writer seeks to understand them by recreating them, but instead he creates them anew. The reader mimics the writer's experience, meeting it in the sensuous word, but then goes on to envision his particular version of it through the variegations of his own stained glass. When one learns the creative trick, reading becomes active, and the range of the book is extended by the reader's experience. In sharing his world, Nabokov appeals not to any sham reality reflected in the communal eye to which he refers in *Pale Fire* but to the special reality created by artist and reader together. In fact, Nabokov discounts any possibility of objective reality, which would reduce whatever is perceived to the flatness of a photograph or the spareness of an outline. The objective vision, while professing detachment and impersonality, stops far short of the gradual accumulation of information which in Nabokov's view constitutes reality, for it lacks the penetration into detail which only a personal perspective, an acknowledged point of view, a position, can give. Interviewed by Nicholas Garnham, Nabokov said, ''Average reality begins to rot and stink as soon as the act of individual creation ceases to animate a subjectively perceived texture,'' and that act of creation may be writing, reading, or simply reflecting. Further, by adding his own information and perspective to that which the artist has accumulated, the reader contributes to the understanding of the reality sought by art.

Like his living metaphors for time in *Ada,* the qualities which inform Nabokov's writings have substance drawn from the actual world of the senses, which must be thoroughly involved if the mind is to create anything which other minds in other bodies can comprehend. The mystery of art's ability to unite is illumined by the senses, for point of view refracts into sensuous knowledge; the body is art's most enduring constant. At his best Nabokov evokes a state of being in which the reader participates sensuously through imagination and thus also shares the writer's sense of mystery. Nabokov shows an uncanny ability to make the reader participate in the experience of the book, to elicit those tears and shivers which, as he says in the Lectures, reveal ''an artistic harmonious balance between the reader's mind and the author's mind.'' He elicits the reader's empathy (both emotional and physical, and the emotional through the physical) through the sublime elaboration of detail. Senses alerted and involved through the minuteness of description, the reader slips across the boundaries of time and space into the world of art. Its appeal is identical to that of the physical world: it animates all the senses. Indeed, by way of a conjurer's trick, the art of transposition in which the performer's hand is far quicker than the audience's eye, Nabokov turns the reader himself into an artist. Giving him materials to work with, showing him how the trick is done, setting the scene, then leaving materials, scene, and action in suspension, Nabokov's fiction requires the reader to become an artist, as William Carroll says. The texture of a text mimes the pattern of life. For ''all of us, everything, is 'authored' in one sense or another. It is the special achievement of Nabokov's fiction that it induces confirmation of this in us, that it represents a confirmation in itself.''

Nabokov's consciousness of the senses and his intellectual refinement make him a writer in whom not only ''average'' readers but also fellow artists find the delight of discovering their own perceptions through his. If Nabokov can please even the most sophisticated reader with the tricks of his art, then the spiral of perception will continue to evolve, and art will be fulfilled through its continuous becoming, its perpetual reaching toward the unattainable, the holy pale fire with which art sanctifies life.

Modernist writers, unable safely to assume values common among themselves and their readers, had to establish bonds with their readers in each work. While Beckett does so by acknowledging the necessity and the uncertainty of existence and Nabokov by observing the details of everyday life, Nin builds her bonds through psychology. Nabokov may abhor psychology as oversimplifying quackery, but Nin celebrates it as an oceanic power that can sweep all people together in mutual understanding. Her reputation as an intimate of her readers tells us how well she succeeded in her literary overtures. While the reader is as implicit a part of her novels as of Nabokov's, little if any similarity exists in the nature of the invitation each extends. Nabokov's is artistic; Nin's is personal. Her Diary attests to the personal hurt she felt when her books were rejected by publishers, harshly reviewed, or ignored. Her art is, simply, an extension of herself.

CHAPTER FOUR

ANAIS NIN

As D. G. James observes, the artist confronts an "illimitable, unplumbed world lying beyond the narrow scope of the discourse of science and the understanding." Anais Nin, however, views this realm not just with the artist's wonder and surmise but with the woman's faith that it can be known, that knowing it will change life radically. For Nin, intuition penetrates where science and rational understanding cannot, and the ultimate discovery is to be found in mankind's collective psyche, awareness of which could enrich human existence with harmony, creative exuberance, and love. Thus, she embarks on a lifelong voyage into the sensual world which, rather than being a distinct phenomenon, she says, exists only in relation to the self, reflecting the depths of the unconscious. For the self, Nin maintains, is the only world; the outer world, its projection. In the psychological climate of her writings, the self is the ultimate mystery; its mastery, the whole mission; relationships, the final meaning; the body, the field of being; analysis and art, complementary keys to understanding the ardors and adversities of life.

In this world, spare of detail yet rich in symbols, only the labyrinthine journey of self-discovery makes awareness possible and action meaningful. Without that, all is flurry and blindness. As each individual probes his interior world, awareness takes root, spreads throughout the human underground, and finally reveals itself as compassionate action—awareness made physical through those who disseminate it with love and care. Unity and meaning begin with the seed, the individual who propagates the collective soul of all who have sought, suffered, and survived.

Nin has written a gospel of the senses, a testament to the creative power of the body and its language, to the physical essence of all abstractions. In her first book, *D. H. Lawrence: An Unprofessional Study* (1932), she revives Lawrence's "plea for whole vision: 'to see with the soul and the body' " and adds her own plea: "to realize philosophy not merely as an intellectual edifice but as a passionate blood-experience." Influenced by Henry Miller, her early prose poem *House of Incest* describes through violent and voluptuous imagery the descent into the psyche. The realism of her Diary records her instantaneous awareness; the symbolism of her novels reflects her law in writing—to reveal "that delicacy and awe of the senses," as she says in the Diary. The novels tell of women in love, and their sexual theme, both literal and symbolic, reflects the inseparable imperatives of sensuous pleasure and spiritual union. Nin's erotica, written in the 1940s and published posthumously as *Delta of Venus* and *Little Birds*, reveals the same sensibility: complex and manifold orgasmic sensations become most compelling—even sacramental—when unleashed by love; but without love, frustrating and incomplete.

But the problem with sensation, Nin suggests, is that it often originates without love, without responsibility, without even awareness. The erotica, written as literary prostitution during hard times, tell mostly of failure, unbridled sensuality leading to madness, frenzy, or despair. Sex without love (including self-love), without understanding, results in alienation, not fulfillment. The heroines of Nin's "continuous novel," *Cities of the Interior,* are sensuous women, but all mistakenly pursue selfish goals—pleasure and identity—through their relationships. Only Lillian in *Seduction of the Minotaur,* an outgrowth of the last of the continuous novels, *Solar Barque,* finally achieves serene and compassionate love, the consummation of eroticism. And only then does she understand her sensuality and make it the real and symbolic nucleus of her union with herself, her husband, and the world.

Sex is virtually a sacrament to Nin, the manifestation of the holy and of values, though not an absolute value in itself. In those terms, only the individual lacking values, lacking the strength of self-knowledge from which values emerge, desires sexual pleasure completely free of sentiment. And such transitory pleasure accents isolation. For, Nin believes, the individual's behavior—and the behavior of others toward him—clearly reveals his inner self, that sole reality. Thus, the pursuit of pleasure without affection betrays psychic and emotional poverty. True sensuality needs awareness; awareness comes from within, confers self-knowledge (or identity) and brings comprehension of the outer world (including the body), of common dreams, of compassion and love. In a final step in this growth of wisdom, life becomes art.

But the journey toward ultimate wisdom is long, and it begins in an arduous struggle to establish identity through action. In the terrestrial analogue to the "real" subterranean world, Nin suggests, deeds merely sublimate and exteriorize the primal instincts, myths, and dreams. Behavior is symbolic; it attempts to define the inner self by means of external acts. In *Seduction of the Minotaur*, for example, Lillian, trying vainly to heal her soul from the outside, changes her environment, runs from an unfulfilling marriage and motherhood to Nin's mythical Mexican city, the golden Golconda, where as a stranger she lacks attachments and is free of customs and expectations. By fleeing, she tries symbolically to declare herself free—only to learn that this very act has merely evaded the psychological need it was intended to allay. In lush Golconda, Lillian fancies herself in tune with her body because she so intensely enjoys the tropical colors, heady aromas, and penetrating warmth of the sun. Yet this exterior beauty and its pleasures are, at first, only symbolic—and symbolic only of her dreams, not of her actuality. Until she frees herself through analysis, even her sensuous experiences remain captive to inhibitions that restrict her imagination and limit her perceptions.

Nin's symbols, whether object or act, are important links between the interior world, which gives them meaning, and the exterior, which gives them form. The interplay is necessary, for, as she says in her theoretical work *The Novel of the Future*, "the unconscious cannot express itself directly because it is a composite of past, present, future, a timeless alchemy of many dimensions." Only a symbol—expressing a more complex psychological reality, making connections through association, feeling, memory, fantasy, even intellect—can convey all these possibilities at once. While symbols connote abstractions, they are highly sensuous in their manifestations and ultimately in their meanings, for they recall the instincts and perceptions of the body that generated them.

Most of Nin's writings, including her Diary, symbolize via person, place, or behavior the search for identity—the force that impels one's life, yet without great effort on the seeker's part remains unknown. The mysterious, shadowy interior, though unseen, is more real than the visible, for it is in fact the force that sees, distorts, mirrors, and designs the raw materials of the outer world according to its own needs and turns the world into a sign of the self.

But this self by which all else is determined is, to most, a complete enigma, perhaps because its dimensions are infinite, its relationships intricate. The discovery of this ultimate mystery is, to Nin, the secret of joy, of love, of union with the world. The self, located within the very soul of humankind, is not singular; it is collective in the broadest sense, not uniform but utterly inclusive of the human whole. Through exploring one's particular self, one discovers the seed of the universal self and achieves the awareness that changes life, gives freedom, and defeats all notions of determinism.

"'Awareness'" is vague, as are many of Nin's other favorite words—
"meaning," "intuition," "dream." Such words encompass so much that
they become hazy. Indeed vagueness seems deliberate with Nin, as though
only thus will her words yield insight universally. As she explains in her
Diary: "My way of working resembles that of a composer of music. I start
from a word or phrase which arouses rich associations, and begin variations
on this, expansions, improvisations. Always in an effort to extract the
largest possible meaning." Further, in a poetic mode Nin often attempts to
bypass the rational dimension of language in favor of the rhythm and image
of words—the magic. By inviting the reader's senses and imagination into
the rhythms and images of her prose, she tries to involve the reader more
directly, more sensuously, than ordinary discourse does. An art that involves the reader through his senses propagates itself, for involvement is
evolutionary: participation leads to understanding, which leads in turn to
communication through word or act. The senses transcend themselves in art.
The awareness preceding creative action is, for Nin, intuition, which she
defined as the sum of observation—a kind of direct communication between
the senses and the world.

To gain awareness of the self—this is the heart of Nin's message, the
search giving direction to all her novels. Yet the two variables of the exercise
are themselves problems. The self: a compound of unknowns—emotions,
dreams, images, intuition, the elaborate maze of the dark unconscious
gathering meaning by experience and association. Awareness: knowledge—
a journey beginning below and spiraling beyond. "Proceed from the dream
outward," said Jung, and Nin reminds us of it so often she makes it a chapter
title in *The Novel of the Future* and includes it in the index. The importance
Nin places on self-discovery cannot be overemphasized. She calls the self
"a conductor of emotion by which we make contact," and "the lens through
which we see others and the world." Without selfhood there would be no
relationships, no art, no meaning.

A quest for meaning may seem anachronistic in a century denied the
luxury of absolutes of any kind, but Nin's world, though not one of
absolutes, is one where recognition of values is integral to serenity. Her
characters have an organic sense of right that flourishes as they do, stings
them with guilt when they languish. As her world is, in this sense, moral, so
does her writing constitute, in the words of Wayne McEvilly, "a literature of
bread, a work which feeds the soul." In his essay "The Two Faces of Death
in Anais Nin's *Seduction of the Minotaur*," he suggests that a quest for
meaning may be utterly imperative in a relativistic universe which would
sunder all human connections unless man strains to hold them together.
McEvilly says:

Our age has forgotten this, the ancient and indeed sacred role of the artist, who brings us the bread which nourishes and sustains, the bread which is the wafer, the symbol, the cipher, that which we absolutely require if we are not to be lost in the ever expanding regions of the space which life reveals to us as we move on toward the ultimate dispersion.

But dispersion is impotent against the one phenomenon that seems, in both Nin's Diary and her fiction, to embody all meaning, all purpose, all reason for living. That phenomenon is relationship: human contact, empathy, understanding, love, drawing dispersion into wholeness, transforming individuals and the world. Relationship is the "outward" toward which one proceeds from the dream along the way to self-realization. Its achievement is the outcome of growth, expansion, unification and its opposite, alienation, is the result of separation, she claims in *The Novel of the Future*. Art itself embodies relationship, the shared body created by both artist and audience. Despite an obvious connection with things outside the self, relationship depends completely on self-knowledge and emotional health, as well as on the willingness to give of the self. As Nin found when she published her Diary, giving of the self means expansion, not loss. Her discovery is recorded in *A Woman Speaks: The Lectures, Seminars and Interviews of Anais Nin*:

> I made several discoveries when I opened it up and when I let it go, when I shared it. But the major one was that relationship was impossible unless one gave the most secret and the deepest part of oneself. . . .And finally this secret self got strong enough so that I reached a certain point. . .where I felt I could face the world with it . . . .Instead of finding myself destroyed, I found the beginning of communion with the whole world.

To attain relationship, then, one must first journey inward to reach, discover, and know the dream that informs a life. The inward route, impeded by fears, social stigmas, self-doubts, and conflicts, follows a labyrinth terrifying in its false leads and dead ends, deception and despair. Yet all its secrets were hidden by the very self who is trying to uncover them. Indeed, these are the only secrets—those hidden from oneself and used for self-delusion. The ego dons a disguise, then does not recognize itself in the mirror.

Relationship also needs responsibility and action—it must be created—otherwise it remains merely abstract. It begins with construction of the self into a serene being with the self-transcendent capacity to care. "What you accomplish alone and what you have to do first of all is to *exist*, to *be*, so that you can be then a friend or a lover or a mother or a child," Nin said in a lecture. The individual is thus responsible for the strength and quality of the relationship, for the love needed to animate and consecrate it. Her emphasis on care and love shows Nin's concern in a fragmented world to accept responsibility for others as well as for herself. Lack of responsibility is Lillian's flaw as *Seduction* opens; acceptance of responsibility as she returns home changes and fulfills her. Responsibility is critically linked to self-discovery, which is the first step toward responsible action. Reaching her psychic depths, she discovers communal dreams, desires, and needs that enable her to understand and care for others. "From the dream outward" thus means from unconsciousness to conscience. Nin says in her *Diary*, "If all of us acted in unison as I act individually there would be no wars and no poverty. I have made myself personally responsible for the fate of every human being who has come my way."

If the senses constitute a way of knowing, they are also instrumental in feeling responsibility. Perception begins sensuously before it is abstracted into an ethic—the urge to care for those whose needs one has perceived. To comprehend this duty beyond the self, one refers to one's own senses; one takes care of another from an empathetic motive—identification with the needs that require attention. Identification and empathy, as Nin writes in *The Novel of the Future*, "bring one inside a human being." Satisfaction of physical needs often creates emotional attachments, as a mother's nursing a child creates an affectional bond. Then, beyond the physical and emotional, care acquires a values connotation, a sense of rightness which determines action (and if one fails then to act he may well suffer guilt and/or confusion). The value both grows out of the physical and emotional dimensions and reinforces them. A certain amount of self-interest remains even in the most self-denying affirmation of a value. (One may die for freedom because to live without it would mean intolerable suffering, either physical or psychological.) But that simply validates the fundamental origin of the value—in the body.

Nin impresses the reader with the importance of the body chiefly through language which constantly attaches positive value to sensuous experience. She says in the Diary, for example, that "the life of the senses, of feeling would lead us back to wholeness." To write sensuously, using the abstraction of language to express direct experience, is to alchemize the mind into the senses, an alchemy expressed in the word for the setting of *Seduction,* the tropics. The word "tropic," signifying change, epitomizes the meaning of the novel, in which Lillian's desired change is just such an alchemy, a fusion of mind and body.

Nin once said that D. H. Lawrence's language "makes a physical impression because he projected his physical response into the thing he observed.'' In accord with her contention that the external world simply mirrors the internal, Nin too describes external phenomena by means of internal reaction. Thus, sensuous language necessarily draws its images from the unconscious to fuse art and life, bypassing the intellect. Such language, as Nin says in *The Novel of the Future,* ''acts more like our life experiences, which enter the body directly before we are able to dissect them.'' Nin even goes so far as to call poetry our relation to the senses, the alchemical agent that converts the raw materials of our fundamental, sensuous experiences into the gold of feelings, creations and ideals, whereby we commune with the world.

Of Nin's many examples of sensuous writing, the most successful evoke an enormous range of human experience—mythic, historical, psychological, artistic—and combine a vivid particularity with a universal pulse. The intensity of this combination, as in this passage from *Seduction,* yields the force of an orgasm:

> In the morning it was the intense radium shafts of the sun on the seas that awakened her, penetrating the native hut. The dawns were like court scenes of Arabian magnificence. The tent of the sky took fire, a laminated coral, dispelling all the sea-shell delicacies which had preceded the birth of the sun, and it was a duel between fire and platinum. The whole sea would seem to have caught fire, until the incendiary dawn stopped burning. After the fire came a rearrangement of more subtle brocades, the turquoise and the coral separated, and transparencies appeared like curtains of the sheerest sari textiles . . . .
>
> Just as music was an unbroken chain in Golconda, so were the synchronizations of color. Where the flowers ended their jeweled displays, their pagan illuminated manuscripts, fruits took up the gradations. Once or twice, her mouth full of fruit, she stopped. She had the feeling that she was eating the dawn.

All the senses are brought into play. For the ears there is music; for the touch, luxurious fabrics; for the nostrils, the intoxicating aroma of tropical flowers; for the tongue, the exotic flavor of native fruits; and for the eyes, the brilliant and harmonious hues, reflections, and forms. Implicit is Nin's belief that if this is available, life is indeed splendid. Only art could put it all together; only life could contain it.

Nin views the senses as the source of all that gives life meaning, from the pleasure they provide to the dreams and symbols they generate, the relationships they incite, and the consequent responsibilities. Beyond these marvels is man's grasp for the infinite, itself made palpable through two phenomena given substance by the senses—art and love. The senses are magnetic, attracting the world to the body, where it is recreated as a personal universe. This reshaping may be orderly or chaotic, may satisfy or terrify according to the order within the individual. If he has not found the thread through his labyrinth, discovered its corners and crevices, he will have trouble finding a place for the world within himself.

But the senses serve only as the point of departure. Until the world is exquisitely perceived, it cannot be profoundly understood. Similarly, unless one knows one's body he will understand little else about himself. For all human faculties grow out of the sensuous self, where experience begins: transcendence evolves from sense. (In her Diary, Nin even wonders ''whether our art concepts were born from some mysterious source such as the designs of our blood cells.'') Phenomenological materials are needed for genius and energy. Without the senses there would be no memory (nor anything to remember), no thought (nor anything to think about), no emotions (nor anything to feel), no imagination (nor any dream to create).

Because Lillian is the only one of Nin's heroines to follow the process of self-discovery to its end—balance and union—*Seduction of the Minotaur* best illustrates the nature of Nin's vision, a scheme that begins with sensuality made barren by self-deception and self-obsession, grows laboriously into self-scrutiny, flourishes as understanding, responsibility, and love, and finally emerges in a renewed and sacred eroticism, unity of self and world. But the journey, long and difficult, begins in an obscurity which overshadows Golconda's bright sun, in Lillian's dim, cold labyrinth. *Seduction* opens with her dream of straining to propel a ship through city streets, a dream that demands contradiction as she struggles to push the barque toward the sea. Both this nightmare and the urgency of contradicting it, motivating her to flee and precipitating the events of the book, reveal her compulsive struggle against herself. Evading the murmur of her internal river (continuity, serenity, wholeness), she embarks on an arid quest for support for her burden. The real solution, of course, the river which can transport the ship of her life naturally and easily, is inside her. That is what she needs to discover and what *Seduction* is all about.

As Lillian arrives in Golconda, she is self-hypnotized, mesmerized by the pleasures of the place into believing she has discovered her true being and milieu at last. Golconda is a sensual paradise, a land alchemized by the sun into gold, rich with color, warmth, and light. As each of the senses is courted seductively and aesthetically by the environment, Lillian becomes intoxicated with the promiscuity, the voluptuousness of her surroundings, where man and nature harmonize in a synaesthetic concert of flowers and colors, music and flavors. Her passion in discovering Golconda is abundant and indiscriminate. On her arrival, she feels she has entered a world of no time but the present, where the immediate is so overwhelming it leaves room for nothing else.

Yet Lillian's abandonment to the beauty of Golconda seems incomplete and artificial. The clues begin in the first paragraph. There is something forced about her presence here, about her journey beginning "in the urgency of contradicting a dream." There is something tarnished in the land of gold—a gold symbolizing not only the golden age but also the fool's gold. There is something potentially dangerous in the atmosphere in which float the vapors of a drug of forgetfulness. And there is something myopic about Lillian's view of the place, especially compared to the insight of Doctor Hernandez, who knows Golconda well, who becomes her mentor, who gives his life for the place, its people, and in a sense for her. Looking at the natives, Lillian sees them impersonally, as objets d'art, ornaments, or pieces of sculpture, not as human beings. She looks at a group of children and sees them "delicately molded...finely chiseled...tender and fragile and neat. The Doctor saw them ill."

Lillian lacks the depth that would allow her to recognize her relationship with the common soul of human beings, the common essence of things. Her senses are keen but dependent and superficial, for she has not generated beauty out of herself. The life she tries to convince herself is real in Golconda is a self-indulgent life, at times a pleasant life, but not one that gives pleasure: it is without meaning. In going to Golconda, Lillian has sought meaning where it cannot be found, in alienation and denial of her responsibilities. She abuses her senses, using them as agents of her denial, as aids to forgetting. At its best, Lillian's sensuality is a source of joy, of a more flowing life, of awareness. But at its most dangerous—isolated from care and reflectiveness—it is a barrier to awareness. Like the mind, the body can be a prison. Unless magnified by the other dimensions of human potentiality (which, in turn, it intensifies), it is self-limiting and insignificant.

Lillian tries to free her sensuality from the burden of thought. Once she walks to the beach and yields herself to the sea's embrace. She seduces herself into feeling reborn, washed free of her past; and she dreams naively of an idealistic, primitive life. But her hope to feel no contradictions ever again is childishly simplistic. And her insistence that she has closed the eyes of memory is repeated many times. Like an incantation, it becomes increasingly meaningless as her memory reveals itself very much awake. There is no distinction between the eyes of memory and Lillian's physical eyes. This one pair of eyes determines her perspective on both past and present; and if the past is blurred, so will be the present. Lillian must bring into focus the double exposure created by memory before she sees her whole life clearly.

Lillian is not only sensuous but also conscious of her senses. Consciousness inscribes her experience on her memory, enriching memory with associative powers, feeding her imagination and her creativity. Because of consciousness, Lillian cannot become a primitive who is merely sensuous— unless she defies the art which is her nature, which gives her life meaning, which her consciousness has generated. She has already shed the primitive sensual life in outgrowing a former lover, Jay, the painter who circumscribed his talent by reducing his vision to the literal, divorcing nature from beauty. His is a "universe of mere BEING, where one lives like a plant, instinctively." Jay declares, "I want just the joy of illumination, the joy of what I see in the world. Just to receive vibrations....Just BE. That was always the role of the artist, to reveal the joy, the ecstasy." Yet his grotesques convey "*his* inability to love...*his* hatred," reducing everything "to acts. He could not understand atmospheres, moods, mysteries." His vision, his life, his art, all lack depth. Inhabiting "a child's world, depending on others' care, others' devotions, others' taking on the burdens," Jay is the polar opposite of Doctor Hernandez, who assumed more responsibility than he had to.

Doctor Hernandez embodies human responsibility. The pensive physician administers to the needs, fights both the illness and the ignorance of the careless Golcondans. His presence in Golconda is explained by his acceptance of awareness and the responsibilities it entails. As he tells Lillian, young Mexican medical students are required to practice for a year in a small town. Though at first he resented caring for the illiterate fishermen and spent his time reading French novels and dreaming of city life, gradually he came to love them and chose to stay. Indeed, his words illuminate the difference between the self-indulgent art suggested by the French novels and the life which is itself a form of art, the embodiment of meaning. Seen with Lillian's eyes, Doctor Hernandez is a sorrowful figure, his black valise a weighty burden. Yet his sorrows signify a profound mystery of almost religious quality. Indeed, Nin ascribes to him the religious roles of both spiritual teacher and sacrificial lamb. But his abstraction of care into compassion and even salvation begins in his senses, as Lillian realizes: "He was suffering and it was this which made him so aware of others' difficulties."

The word "aware" is often connected with Doctor Hernandez, a doctor who deals in awareness. To dispense it is his duty, his goal. And he knows he will be punished, for people hate awareness. Seeking to expand the instincts through consciousness, the Doctor becomes the enemy of the illegal drug traffickers who would tame the terrors of awareness, cure the pain of knowledge and memory. His refusal to collaborate with them finally results in his death; he is shot by the enemies of awareness who propose to profit from the Golcondans' resignation and fatalism.

But his death, shocking Lillian into reflection and action, is her salvation. Stunned to realize that Doctor Hernandez "had wanted, needed all the care he gave," Lillian no longer delays confronting the minotaur that devours her heart. For she knows that even Doctor Hernandez, lacking the intimacy she might have supplied, had not been able to escape the truth of his own warning:

> We may seem to forget a person, a place, a state of being, a past life, but meanwhile what we are doing is selecting a new cast for the reproduction of the same drama, seeking the closest reproduction to the friend, the lover, or the husband we are striving to forget. And one day we open our eyes, and there we are caught in the same pattern, repeating the same story. How could it be otherwise? The design comes from within us. It is internal.

This pattern is the labyrinth (elsewhere called by Nin *l'origine de l'esprit*), the design of one's interior being which projects itself on the outer world. At its center is the minotaur, the secret self one fears to face. Stymied by fear, one wanders aimlessly in the maze, making the same mistakes again and again. Lillian must seduce the minotaur, entice it into the light where she can recognize it, before she can achieve balance and union.

Until this point Lillian has followed the labyrinth around and around the central issue—her own being—without finding it. Deliberately taking wrong turns to avoid the minotaur, she has recognized and rejected this very weakness in others: Hatcher, for example, proclaims his freedom from his native America simply by virtue of having emigrated to Mexico, but he shows a pathetic dependence by hoarding American goods. And Michael inhabits a ruined city where his cold homosexuality is not judged deviant because he is the only judge. These Lillian can analyze until at last, by extension, she can also analyze herself. She walks in the common world of dreams and fears and recognizes them as her own.

By rejecting the self-indulgent, deathlike world of Michael and accepting the human world of responsibility, Lillian comes to terms with her past, uses it to understand herself and to advance. She realizes that her flight to Golconda had not been the independent act she believed it to be but an impulse from her unresolved past which, like a broken record, replays the familiar phrase until she corrects it. Lillian achieves resolution by seeing the drama of her experiences in Golconda, the cast of characters she has chosen for it, simply as a road show of her life in New York. She has behaved and selected her companions symbolically—for their resemblance to someone familiar. Her husband Larry was present in the "prisoner" for whom Lillian naively paid bail; in her young, innocent friend Christmas; in Lillian herself, who impersonated her husband by adopting his values and judgments toward people in Golconda, seeing them only as children or animals (for which Larry had a weakness) and not as complete human beings.

In recognizing the human fact of responsibility, Lillian acquires a transcendent vision, adds sense to her senses, thought to her hitherto compulsive physicality. She realizes that nothing is as it seems, that even the pure sensuality she imagined among the natives is only an illusion. The passionate will for oblivion behind their apparent sensuality is symbolized in their violence against Doctor Hernandez—the suffering desperation that compelled their craving for the drug of forgetfulness.

Why is this understanding given to Lillian? The knowledge she attains is more emotional than intellectual, very much a part of the concept of feeling, including both senses and emotions—or, more particularly, emotional release through sensuous awareness. In *The Novel of the Future* Nin explains that Lillian is the only one of her four heroines in *Cities of the Interior* to achieve fusion and balance because "she was the only one who could receive the eloquent messages direct from nature. Through the senses (which she feared to yield to sensually) she was able to become at one with nature (her nature) through the Doctor's insights.'" As Evelyn Hinz points out in *The Mirror and the Garden*, Lillian becomes self-aware through "her reconciliation of conscience and impulse,'" through "recognition and appreciation of her body and sexual appetites'" as well as "her willingness to accept her conscience and the consequent obligations.'" Emerging from the harmony of senses and emotions is a communal and metaphysical unity that generates compassion and creativity.

Nin explores the interdependence of the physical and the metaphysical in *Seduction* through one of the senses, sight, whose power and penetration increase as the book moves toward resolution. Simple seeing evolves into observation, insight, reflection, and vision as Lillian herself changes. On her arrival in Golconda she is quickly aware of the natives' laughing eyes, their candid stares, their physical vision. Overtly she responds, for, as the opposite of everything against which she is rebelling, this openness is just what she has sought. In Golconda, she believes, sight is remarkably clear. Unlike the white man with his vision mediated by glasses, cameras, and telescopes, the natives commune directly with eyes and smiles.

The virtue of direct vision is reinforced by its contrast with various forms of blindness in the novel's self-limiting characters: Hatcher's dark glasses, Michael's ruined city where there is virtually nothing to see. But the natives' immediacy of vision is not entirely positive. They stare like children and animals; they see only the present. Lillian is not a child, and more than the present determines her life. She needs a mature perspective on the world and her own history if she would shape her life. Or else, "'One day we open our eyes, and there we are caught in the same pattern.''

The eye opener for Lillian is another pair of eyes—a child's—as she rides a bus to visit Hatcher. The child has eyes ''so large that it seemed she must see more than anyone, and reveal more of herself than any child.'' Lillian calls her the transparent child, who displays open naked feelings and thoughts. As the bus, with metaphorically appropriate timing, passes through a tunnel, the image of the child fades in Lillian's mind into the image of herself as a child. It is her first effort to recall what she has been trying to obliterate, the first step toward awareness. Even in her childhood, Lillian remembers, the eyes that had determined her image of herself were not her own but her mother's, critical, cold, and forbidding her to display her feelings. Lillian is released by the realization that she has never really looked at herself through her own eyes. Although she later tries again to shut the eyes of memory, they will not be closed now that they have begun the wondrous experience of seeing. And once she looks clearly at herself she is freed of the wild swings of temperament that had controlled her. She gains serenity, a sense of continuity, as she examines one by one the moving forces of her life. She surveys the labyrinth, finds the minotaur, which can no longer terrify. The eye imagery culminates as Lillian looks at the minotaur she had so long feared and finds it ''not a monster. It was a reflection upon a mirror, a masked woman, Lillian herself, the hidden part of herself unknown to her, who had ruled her acts.''

Seeing herself clearly, Lillian decides to return to Larry, for ''she now knew her responsibility in the symbolic drama of their marriage.'' She will complement Larry, who has tended toward too great austerity, reservation, hesitation, fear. *Seduction* ends firmly on the conviction that love is salvation, the ultimate attainment of two human beings united in body, mind, and soul. But this metaphysical union begins with the body, the source of energy, the attraction that pulls the rest together:

> Her vehement presence became the magnet. She summoned him back from solitude . . . .He was truly born in her warmth and her conviction of his existence . . . .

> Lillian felt that in the husband playing the role of husband, in the scientist playing his role of scientist, in the father playing his role of father, there was always the danger of detachment. He had to be maintained on the ground, given a body. She breathed, laughed, stirred, and was tumultuous for him. Together they moved as one living body and Larry was passionately willed into being born, this time permanently.

The dialogue between interior and exterior in *Seduction* is like a swinging pendulum, like Lillian's vacillation between the drug of awareness and the drug of forgetfulness. Uncontrolled by her whose life it ticks off, it is wild, tumultuous, disruptive, leaving the individual at the mercy of its erratic momentum. In balance, however, it originates a dialectic of growth and change toward wholeness. Having faced the minotaur, Lillian can close the eyes of memory without blinding herself or being doomed to repetition; memory will not clamor for attention, will not invade the dream life, will not rule the unconscious, but will merge into Lillian's consciousness, subsumed into the whole, quietly a part of her at last. She has successfully married conscience—her past, sense of responsibility, and guilt—with impulse—her abundant feelings and sensuousness. The renewal of her marriage is an appropriate metaphor for the unity of opposites she achieves.

If Lillian depended on nature—the exterior realm—for stimulation and vision at the beginning of *Seduction,* she draws on her own more fecund vision at the end. Since love turns everything into gold, as Nin says in the Diary, she no longer needs the golden land. The blankness of the view outside the portholes of the airplane traveling home contrasts sharply with the lavish colors, intense sunlight, heady scents, and music of Golconda; yet Lillian's imagination conjures richer scenery—not only the past, which she ponders and resolves, but a future of wholeness and joy. She has absorbed all time, transcended it through knowledge that the present is not the absence of past and future but their composite. Living in the present is entirely different from how Lillian had imagined it would be. This present is the fullness of time, not its negation. A new sense must evolve to comprehend this startling and wonderful immediacy—a sense to perceive shadows and resonances as well as phenomena, a sense to forecast change, follow flux, defy the dictates of form. For Lillian this metasense is love, sanctifying the body and giving birth to the soul. For Nin her creator it is also art—"the high moment of fusion . . .a sense of communion with the universe,"as she words it in the Diary—an art of relativity, eternal flux; an art of compassion as well, a literature of bread.

Orville Clark holds that *Seduction* is the height of erotic development in Nin's writings because eroticism is transformed into compassion, "and finally compassion results in that 'miraculous openness of love' and the fulfillment of one's being." Indeed, Clark continues:

> *Seduction of the Minotaur* might best be described as a kind of "phenomenology of care": that is as a study of the essence of compassionate love. But this is not a disembodied or other worldly essence; it is a fully sensuous and concrete, a fully *embodied* eros . . .the sensuous body itself—a body capable of loving and giving without guilt. This body is that visible link between the

conscious and the unconscious, between dream and reality: The sensuous body *is* the visibility of human eros.

The embodied eros realized only near the end of her career as a novelist is Nin's fullest representation of what D. G. James calls metasensual: the body merges with the beyond, manifests the beyond. Between real and ideal, self and other, inner and outer worlds, indeed, there is no distinction.

Figuratively picking up where *Seduction* leaves off, *Collages* exemplifies, in its spare and curious and understated way, an art of compassion, an almost egoless art. Its leading character, Renate, is the woman Lillian was becoming—one who knows herself, is on intimate terms with the world, and feels concern for everyone she meets. But she is more the artist than Lillian, for her detachment from herself, a spiritual freedom, releases her imagination. Observing the world intently, concentrating her energies in it, she cannot help transforming her observations into creations. In her essay "The Poetic Reality of Anais Nin," Anna Balakian writes:

> There is a marvelous juxtaposition possible between *Seduction of the Minotaur* and *Collages. Seduction* presents a landscape of gold, exterior to the viewer, and which becomes monotonous and inert for those who merely pass through it. In *Collages,* the golden landscapes are produced from within, and therefore their impact is dynamic and contagious. Golconda is metaphorically speaking the divinity of nature; in *Collages* Anais Nin's parable of the writer who meets the incarnation of one of his characters brings into focus the universal truth of the relationship essential between the outer world and the artist's inner one.

As *Seduction* progresses toward a sort of death, annihilation of the old self, *Collages* follows the life after death—ephemeral and free. The senses are borne lightly as though by a breeze, not confined by the body's weight. And while *Seduction* follows a sequence of events, *Collages* consists of interchangeable parts. Thus, *Seduction* necessarily pursues its own inevitable logic, while *Collages* breaks free of chronological and spatial boundaries. (Renate simply appears in a new place; she doesn't travel to it. Lillian makes all the efforts of a journey, takes planes and buses, packs suitcases.) As the title suggests, *Collages* is a montage, made up of fables about people whose inner lives are strong—so strong, in fact, that they may overshadow outer reality. Isolated in their private fantasies, they are nevertheless loosely united through Renate who, making no demands herself, draws them out. She is secure enough to receive others on their own terms, to do without preconceptions. That is to say, she is an artist—in a Joycean sense—refined out of existence, a transparent medium through which others are apparent. It is not that Renate lacks an inner life, but, as Nin said of the real woman who served as a model for the fictional character, she penetrates any experience or role without dissolution of her self. In fact, she generates the personages of *Collages* out of her rich inner life. She nurtures relationships with those who, like the statues in her native Vienna, seem fixed and inert by day but by night come magically to life as the incarnation of dreams. Recognizing these beings, she makes them real, gives them a place in the world, thus verifying her own inner life as well as theirs. Renate's artistic, almost psychic impulse assumes a sensuous form.

Projection of dreams gives her a more than circumstantial interest in the reality so created, and her perceptions are finely attuned to the miracle. Her senses are primed to experience actively this vivid and exciting world of their own making. Thus, while the characters of *Collages* may seem out of touch with conventional expectations and behavior, they are more literally—sensually—"in touch" than the conventional individual. Deena Metzger, reviewing *Collages* in the Los Angeles *Free Press,* says:

> . . .although *Collages* is a novel about people with dreams they are people who are connected to the world through a thousand sensual links and whose dreams are made manifest by a multiplicity of acts and gestures. *Collages* is premised on the observation that there is a symbolic relationship between a person's inner life and his gestures. The secret thoughts and dreams of the characters spill out through their fingers and define them.

The character best embodying this idea is Nina Gitana de la Primavera, the spritelike creature who is flux itself and speaks the language of mythology: "I change with the seasons. When the spring comes I no longer need to be Primavera." But along with her ephemeral, evocative language she maintains a curious earthiness, Ophelia-like, yielding. Even the abstraction of language becomes physical by her sensuous appreciation of it, as though she caresses words while uttering them.

But her gestures keep Nina from vanishing into a melody of words. Seeing, touching, tasting, she affirms her substance, her reality. Talking with Renate and Bruce, she touches their faces delicately; attending a play in which the actors eat, she takes out a sandwich and a pickle and begins to eat in unison, so that the actors will feel less lonely. For Nina the senses are the prime source of human contact, and not just of physical contact. Since her esoteric mind is inaccessible to most, she needs to confirm her reality through gestures that allow her to communicate without submitting to convention. As in *Seduction,* the body is the magnet by which the inner self attracts. Nina's sensuous nature is at one with her inner being, which it manifests, and she uses her body to establish connection with kindred spirits. Through her body, her spirit transforms the people and places where she alights.

Like Nina, Count Laundromat (a laundromat owner) has transformed the world according to his inner perspective. Instead of using his mundane life as an excuse for mediocrity, he exploits his vibrant imagination to make an apparently ordinary life unique and fascinating. Count Laundromat draws on the sensuous present—that which is actual and immediate—to create a life entirely different from the one he leads on the surface. The trivial becomes grand, aristocratic, artistic, almost mythic by the way his inner self transsubstantiates it. Sheets are treated like lace; money, like a bouquet. Converting everyday chores into experiences to be savored, the Count establishes a link with Renate, who appreciates both the attitude and the experience. What could be drudgery becomes a fellowship of heightened awareness: "They agreed that if human beings had to attend to soiled laundry, they had been given, at the same time, a faculty for detaching themselves, not noticing, or forgetting certain duties and focusing on how to enhance, heighten, add charm to daily living."

When they discover a shared childhood (the Count had come from a noble family of Vienna, Renate's city), their link becomes even stronger, more sensual, the past dissolving in the present. Memory, with its power to alchemize events into poetry, turns the past into a timeless yet palpable present, so that, for Renate, the Count's laundromat can never be just a place to wash clothes but becomes a time capsule to an eternal world of perception and feeling. The smells of the laundromat—detergent and wet fabrics— merge with the smells of an antique cabinet—rose petals, sandalwood, spices—and yield to the seductive power of beauty. Deeper than the odors of detergents and dirty clothes are the intoxicating scents and senses of memory, suffused with fantasies and reveries. More lasting than drudgery are dreams, transforming labor into pleasure. More real than everyday is forever, the timelessness of imagination. Laundered in the Count's machines, dull materials emerge as fine tissues of beauty and wonder, intricate weavings of art and love. For the Count's links with humanity are not his common and mundane chores, transitory and monotonous, but his transformation of them into noble deeds, through memory, imagination, dream. His story establishes him as an artist of the inner world where identities merge.

The weaving of disparate experiences into the cloth of art is most clearly represented in the portrait of Varda, the collage maker, "the alchemist searching only for what he could transmute into gold." He resides in a converted ferry boat (representing motion and passage), and his work embodies change, flux, evolution—rags into the riches of art. Varda makes his raw materials, scraps and bits of cloth, into an artistic fabric whose whole is more than the sum of its parts. Only imagination can comprehend its complexity, for the senses are perplexed (though pleased) by its synaesthetic profusion. Without sacrificing the integrity of each sense, Varda entices all of them into his collage, composing the senses symphonically. In their intensity, in their permutations and dynamics, Varda's collages surpass nature, astonish their audience into awareness of the superreality of myths, dreams, and the never-never land of fantasy. They outshine the sun, dim the sea, breathe and pulsate like living bodies. And like life they change, move, transform themselves.

But their very evanescence, their mutability, permits his collage women to endure, floating in space, free of restrictions, changing with time, inviting a Babel of interpretations, a kaleidoscope of viewpoints. As Varda tells his daughter, "What I wanted to teach you is contained in one page of the dictionary. It is in all the words beginning with *trans*: transfigure, transport, transcend, translucent, transgression, transform, transmit, transmute, transpire, all the trans-Siberian voyages." Nin herself has frequently asserted that "trans" words suggest the very role of art and the key to life—to change and to make changes, to be free of circumstances and expectations, to mold them to one's vision of the desirable and the possible.

Varda maintains that nothing endures "unless it has first been transposed into a myth, and the great advantage of myths is that they are ladies with portable roots." As Oliver Evans points out in his *Anais Nin* Renate herself is such a lady, both mobile and transparent. While, like a collage, she encapsulates and animates the stories as she passes through them, she also lets the reader see the tales clearly through her. Each story remains individual despite their common myth, Renate, who finds in each a manifestation of her inner self.

Other characters, however, lack an outer complement to their inner worlds. Each faces a limitation. Varda has a sullen, unattractive daughter who appreciates his work only after taking drugs. Count Laundromat has a fat, irritable wife whose demands confine him to one city. Nobuko, the Japanese actress, is a slave to tradition and symbols; she cannot write letters on a rainy day unless she has pearl gray paper to match. And Bruce, Renate's sometime lover, has the frustrations of narcissism.

Renate remains human through her sorrows, particularly over Bruce's homosexual infidelity. Nevertheless, she transcends most human limitations through self-knowledge and flux. Evans maintains that she does not change during the book; but one who is, as Varda puts it, "*femme toute faite . . .* already designed, completed, perfect in every detail," has no need to change. Lillian, on the other hand, was confused and diffident; her metamorphosis was essential. Yet Renate does change in ways that matter to Nin. Like a rapid river, she is constantly in motion, reflecting the world around her as water refracts the sun. She is ready for new experiences, tries new things, always seeks to expand her world. In doing so, she connects the other characters of *Collages* with the rest of the world.

Evans considers Renate a rather weak link for the several stories of *Collages*. Yet in a critical way the novel is, after all, Renate's story. Not only does she begin and end the book, but, without the obvious limitations of the other characters, she also provides a model of the whole, happy, and creative individual. By not detailing Renate's life, Nin implies that Renate transcends the particularities and trivialities of biography. We can know her partly through the people she meets, whose existence she internalizes. Sometimes a waitress, she inspires even her customers with her singular energy:

> "Renate," they called, not because they were hungry or thirsty, but because she knew who she was, and as she knew who she was, she might also be able to identify them, with a smile and a word, just as with a smile and a word she had said to Bruce: "You are a poet." ... Renate was more than a woman, she was a compass.

She confers identity not by analyzing people but by merging her buoyant unconscious with their inhibited ones, dissolving their fears and uncertainties, freeing them to act. Knowing who she is implies, in Nin's psychology, penetrating the mysteries of the self, traversing boundaries, eliminating superficialities. Through the sensuous flow of the unconscious, Renate empathizes with others and becomes them, their balance and their synthesis. She surpasses the conflicts and events of history or biography for the universality of the story, of art. Indeed, "Collages" could be Renate's name, for she is a collage, as are we all: "We are composites in reality," says Nin in *The Novel of the Future*.

Renate's mode of perception is literally com-passion, "passion with," a sharing of sensibilities with those she meets. She is a true human being as Nin defines one, again in *The Novel of the Future*: "What makes us human is empathy, sympathy." And she makes others human, too. The ability to empathize comes from her self-assurance and self-awareness, qualities that help make others comfortable with themselves and that bring out their best, their truth. Her profound awareness of the body and her generous sympathies marry in love and joy and make her a complete woman. Reassuring, warming all who need her, both comforting and exciting them, Renate embodies woman as artist and lover, mother and goddess, creator and sustainer of life. While *Seduction of the Minotaur* ends in an overture to compassionate love, *Collages* carries the melody throughout. Every one of Renate's relationships is born of that sensibility. By feeling as others feel, entering their senses and dreams, she nurtures the highest form of love, one wholly outside the self—the kind of love Lillian was just beginning to imagine. Entering others' fantasies, Renate realizes them. A sick woman rejoices in Renate's confidence that a handsome man had found the woman dangerously enticing. Henri the chef takes comfort in Renate's reassurance that people still appreciate his cooking but that language has grown too poor for them to express it. This is bread for the soul indeed.

Despite the selflessness of Renate's compassion, once cast upon the waters it returns to confirm her own character, her own passions, as well. Doctor Mann, seeking to meet the recluse author Judith Sands, comes to Renate with his story. He has gone to Judith Sands's door and, as she will not let him in, he importunes her with an interminable monologue in which he claims that the novelist is destined to meet the incarnation of at least one of his characters, because the portrait "will draw into its circle those who resemble it." He is, he says, one of her characters. Returning a second day, Doctor Mann argues again at her door until finally she admits him. He tries to prove that she need not shelter herself from the world, for it is, in fact, of her own making: "You and those you loved have children scattered all over the world. They are descendants in direct line from your creations."

When he takes her to witness the machine that destroys itself (the anti-artist's nihilistic invention), they meet Renate. Typically, she is trying to rescue from the clutches of the machine a piano with still a song in it. Judith Sands invites them to her apartment to show them what no one else has seen—her new book. And as Renate reads the first paragraph she finds her own fulfillment, to be created and nurtured and understood as she has done for others. For the character she meets in Judith Sands's book is herself, in a paragraph virtually identical with the one that opens *Collages*:

> Vienna was the city of statues. They were as numerous as the people who walked the streets. They stood on the tip of the highest towers, lay down on stone tombs, sat on horseback, kneeled, prayed, fought animals and wars, danced, drank wine and read books made of stone.

As Renate is thus completed, so is Judith Sands, for her dreams—her imagination and inner self—meet their outer complement in Renate. The unity is total. *Collages* ends as Judith Sands's book opens, continuing the spiral of art.

There is only one word of difference between the opening and closing paragraphs of the novel. The beginning reads, "They stood on the *top* of the highest towers," while Judith Sands's paragraph reads "the tip." That single syllable is tantalizingly disturbing to one who would like the aesthetic satisfaction of a circular book, completely self-contained. But perhaps the modification suggests that as life and art go on together they spiral rather than merely repeat the same pattern. Indeed, "tip," more remote than "top," suggests ascension toward infinity, perhaps toward spiritualization. Like "word golf" in Nabokov's *Pale Fire,* the "top-tip" progression may signal the artist's power to transform language as he transforms life, to make both eternal because of their resilience that allows for evolution and change. Unity means flux, not stasis.

The end of *Collages* evokes a constant theme in Nin's work—the union of life and art. In her Diary she writes, "There is no separation between my life and my craft, my work. The form of the art is the form of art of my life, and my life is the form of the art. I refuse artificial patterns. Stories do not end." In a sense, both *Seduction* and *Collages* do not end but open upon an infinite future of dreams made true. "That union of life and art, that marriage, as of Lillian going home in *Seduction of the Minotaur,*" as Nin put it to an interviewer for *Chicago Review,* and the convergence of Judith Sands's book with Renate's life (and with Anais Nin's book and her life too)—these symbols look beyond the present like classical comedy. The loving atmosphere permeating the final sections of each book radiates joy, gives a sense of the possible in which Nin invites her readers to participate.

Although *Collages* is Nin's last novel, it is not the end of her art. Having struggled through the stages of creativity, she at last reaches the ultimate—creation of herself, of her life as a work of art. Just as all the women of *Cities of the Interior* are superseded by Lillian, the one who discovers her true self, so is Lillian superseded by Renate, the one whose self no longer matters. And Renate, in turn, walks out of fiction and becomes Anais Nin herself—the mature woman no longer needing art as an extension of her identity but turning identity into compassion incarnate. "Proceed from the dream outward" reaches its fullest realization in this transformation of the self into care, embodied eros.

During the last years of her life, Nin carried her discoveries and her compassion to the young by lecturing at colleges. Her recognition among young people seems comparable to the attention Renate won. As models of secure, self-aware, self-transcendent human beings, both are implored to confer identity and inspiration on others. And both can do so, for the artist confers life on others who read themselves in her characters, as Doctor Mann and Renate find themselves in Judith Sands's imagination.

Nin's answer to a question following a lecture (printed in *A Woman Speaks*) reveals the spiritual evolution which began in the dream, from diary to art to transcendent life, life as a collage:

Q. Are you still writing in the diaries?

A. No, and it's your fault. I'm answering letters. But I think that that may be the natural outcome of a diary. I'm not concerned about it because I have received other diaries; I have received letters that are like diaries; I have received very personal confessions and I have answered them. Perhaps that's the ultimate *raison d'être* of the diary: that it ceases to be a solitary occupation and becomes a universal work . . . .

I have talked about the continuity of the diary even though it takes different forms . . . .this year it has become a correspondence with the world, and probably that is the right ending for a diary, that it would start as a river and then flow into an ocean and become an exchange of our more secret and private lives, which is what the letters which I answer are. So I'm not worried about the meta-morphosis of the diary which has now become universal, in other words, which has become *our* diary.

Whatever the critical evaluation of her art, Nin achieves an indisputable triumph at the end of her life. She succeeds in reaching an audience and in outreaching herself, liberating herself through a humanistic love that in-forms and surpasses her art. Responsibility toward those who love her unites her life with theirs, as Lillian's is married with Larry's. Her warmth illumines the shadows of their dreams, their dreams establish the reality of her own, and together they move "as one living body . . .willed into being born."

CHAPTER FIVE

CONCLUSION

The black humor and despair in Beckett's work, love in Nabokov's, compassion in Nin's, all underscore the moral imperatives of human physiology—a sympathetic nerve radiating from self to other and animating the entire network of human consciousness with care. It is in this ethic indeed that the senses become our means of communion and of change; it is in its acknowledgment of the senses and their ethic that art comes to matter.

In saying that "the only chance of renovation is to open our eyes and see the mess," Beckett creates—existentially at least—an obligation for himself: to help his readers see the mess and foresee renovation. This obligation conforms with his primary one, the "obligation to express," so that the form of his art not only manifests the mess but also dimly illumines the remote possibility that the human lot may someday, somehow improve. As Tom Driver rightly observes, Beckett's art is compassionate and his attitude toward his characters affectionate. Yet Beckett avoids paternalism (which would distance both himself and the reader) through an ambiguity which makes the character everyone and no one, the reader and Beckett himself. By shifting or abstracting point of view, Beckett focuses attention on character, the one constant (confused but always there) in a world of fluctuations—a world in which not only point of view but setting, tone, even language may be altered unpredictably. The character, however, is himself abstract, the more so the later one gets into Beckett's oeuvre, where personality is eventually divested altogether. In undressing their bodies and minds, removing the fashion of personality, Beckett makes his characters prototypes of humanity and makes the reader look at them—at the mess of them—honestly.

94

Of course, the attitude engendered by this image is another sort of mess, a confusion of pity and disgust, compassion and disregard, horror and hope, love and hate. But because these feelings cannot be attached to a specific individual, a personality, as easily as they can be in more conventional forms of literature, they are extraordinarily disturbing. For the human prototypes in Beckett's art are not merely man but also, to each reader, himself. Basically, each reader understands man in terms of himself, experiences the confinement of Beckett's people with his own senses and thus at every moment becomes part of the text. His feelings about the character reflect his feelings about himself, magnified to encompass mankind. Both positive and negative emotions are aroused, of course, but in the long run the reader is more likely to develop compassion, which flows from his drive for preservation of the species. Because it is self-referential, the compassion evoked by Beckett's naked image of man tends to outweigh the disgust. At the same time, Beckett avoids engendering self-pity or complacency in the reader because the objectivity of his characters about their own suffering keeps the reader critically detached. The combination of compassion and detachment effects the liberation of which the fizzle is the metaphor: both spirit and body are freed of the inhibitions and pretentions of the ego so that man can acknowledge his situation and his nature at last and perhaps, in going on, finally make some progress.

Involving the reader's sympathies yet keeping him critically reflective, Beckett's art provides a foundation for the renovation of which he speaks. Honesty of vision is the first step, feeling and thought the second, before understanding is reached; and understanding is necessary before positive change comes about. The view may not be good, but it can become better. As the Swedish Academy's secretary said when Beckett was awarded the Nobel Prize in literature in 1969, Beckett's plays and novels contain "a love of mankind that grows in understanding as it plumbs further into the depths of abhorrence."

Not only Beckett's, of course, but all literature gives the reader the materials with which to change life. Certainly Nin's "literature of bread" intends to do just that. "The creative writer is one who teaches expansion and liberation of the human mind," she says in *The Novel of the Future;* and she became her own best example, an artist wholly diffused, at last, in compassion. Nabokov in his very different way gives the reader a glimpse of this same potential, a vista of the infinite reach of the human mind with the freedom to create a universe. For art makes one someone else within himself; it develops his potential to use his senses as a bridge to the other, whom he can then sense as other instead of as an extension or replica of himself. Despite Nabokov's disclaimers as to messages in his writings, there is certainly a lesson of this sort in *Lolita.* Humbert Humbert suffers, for all his artistry, from a myopic imagination that cannot peer beyond its own limits. By the end of the novel he has learned that to "solipsize" the object of desire is not the same as to love her.

Cherishing the other's integrity is a form of love that requires liberating the imagination—another driving force of modernist art. Art cannot, in fact, be separated from a human genius for love: both enable us to feel what the other feels, to imagine the receipt of impulses from the beyond. Even in novels like Anthony Burgess's *A Clockwork Orange* or John Hawkes's *The Blood Oranges,* where the values of the narrator-protagonist (violence in *A Clockwork Orange,* calculated sex in *The Blood Oranges*) are not likely to be those of the reader, the reader is seduced by the narrator, becomes an ally, comes to share the narrator's values as he senses his experiences, partakes of his consciousness (and, indeed, helps to create him). In this extension of his senses and mind, the reader is liberated from his private habits and inhibitions, and when he returns to himself he sees himself with different eyes— the eyes of the other—which may clarify his self-image. Thus, this modernist aesthetic has the effect of an increase in understanding which is both expansive and reflexive. As it unfolds toward the other, so too it enfolds the other unto the self. Concentration on the senses can diffuse consciousness into the whole universe of human intercourse. "For it is as one biological species that mankind is one," writes Brown in *Love's Body.*

The generation of understanding in the reader carries with it an obligation equal to the writer's—to live with that understanding and to make it live. In the work of art, writer and reader converge from points in the real world which would not meet without art's topological sorcery. Many envision this convergence as man's destiny. Brown's resurrection of the body is to be a "union with others and with the world around us based not on anxiety and aggression but on narcissism and erotic exuberance." Octavio Paz's concrete life, discoverable through poetry, will satisfy man's desire "to be one with his creations, to unite with himself and with his fellows, to be the world without ceasing to be himself." Owen Barfield's mystery of the kingdom is to be "a violent change in the whole *direction* of human consciousness" in which "henceforth the life of the image is to be drawn from within. The life of the image is to be none other than the life of the imagination."

The poem is the domain where writer and reader cohabit sacramentally, each responsible to incarnate the word in his own life. The way each lives defines the word, gives meaning to art, and returns, like bread cast upon the waters, to sanctify the body through which life flows. When writer and reader accept the awesome responsibility of art, feel its course through the bloodstream and its strength to evoke unifying values through our very neurology, perhaps art will realize its potential to change life radically, to become life itself. It will be the body resurrected, the figurative become the figure, the poetic life, freedom at last.

BIBLIOGRAPHY

PRIMARY SOURCES

Beckett, Samuel. *Ends and Odds*. New York: Grove Press, 1976.
———. *Fizzles*. New York: Grove Press, 1976.
———. "Hommage à Jack B. Yeats." Trans. Ruby Cohn. In *Jack B. Yeats: A Centenary Gathering*. Dublin: Dolmen, 1971.
———. *How It Is*. New York: Grove Press, 1964.
———. *The Lost Ones*. New York: Grove Press, 1972.
———. *Murphy*. New York: Grove Press, 1957.
———. *Poems in English*. New York: Grove Press, 1961.
———. *Proust*. New York: Grove Press, 1961.
———. *Stories and Texts for Nothing*. New York: Grove Press, 1974.
———. *Three Novels: "Molloy," "Malone Dies," "The Unnamable."* New York: Grove Press, 1965.
———. *Waiting for Godot*. New York: Grove Press, 1954.
———, and Georges Duthuit. *Proust and Three Dialogues*. London: Calder & Boyars, 1965.
Nabokov, Vladimir. *Ada or Ardor: A Family Chronicle*. New York: McGraw-Hill, 1969.
———. *Bend Sinister*. New York: McGraw-Hill, 1973.
———. *Details of a Sunset and Other Stories*. New York: McGraw-Hill, 1976.
———. *The Gift*. New York: Putnam's, 1963.
———. *Invitation to a Beheading*. New York: Putnam's, 1959.
———. *Lectures on Literature*. Ed. Fredson Bowers. New York: Harcourt Brace Jovanovich, 1980.
———. *Lolita*. New York: Putnam's, 1955.
———. *Nikolai Gogol*. New York: New Directions, 1961.
———. *Pale Fire*. New York: Putnam's, 1962.
———. *Poems and Problems*. New York: McGraw-Hill, 1970.
———. *Speak, Memory: An Autobiography Revisited*. New York: Putnam's, 1966.
———. *Strong Opinions*. New York: McGraw-Hill, 1973.
———. *Transparent Things*. New York: McGraw-Hill, 1972.
———. Intro. to and trans. of *Eugene Onegin*, by Aleksandr Pushkin. 4 vols. New York: Bollingen Foundation, 1964.

Nin, Anais. *Collages*. Chicago: Swallow, 1964.

——. *D. H. Lawrence: An Unprofessional Study*. Chicago: Swallow, 1964.

——. *Delta of Venus*. New York: Harcourt Brace Jovanovich, 1977.

——. *The Diary of Anaïs Nin*. 7 vols. New York: Harcourt Brace Jovanovich, 1966–1978.

——. *House of Incest*. Chicago: Swallow, 1958.

——. *The Novel of the Future*. New York: Macmillan, 1968.

——. *Seduction of the Minotaur*. Chicago: Swallow, 1961.

——. *A Woman Speaks: The Lectures, Seminars and Interviews of Anaïs Nin*. Ed. Evelyn J. Hinz. Chicago: Swallow, 1975.

SECONDARY SOURCES

Alvarez, A. *Samuel Beckett*. New York: Viking, 1973.

Auden, W. H. "Greatness Finding Itself." In his *Forewords and Afterwords*. New York: Random House, 1973.

Auster, Paul. "Ending without End." *Saturday Review*, 30 April 1977, pp. 20, 22–23.

Bader, Julia. *Crystal Land: Artifice in Nabokov's English Novels*. Berkeley: University of California Press, 1972.

Bair, Deirdre. *Samuel Beckett*. New York: Harcourt Brace Jovanovich, 1978.

Balakian, Anna. "The Poetic Reality of Anais Nin." Preface to *Anais Nin Reader*, ed. Philip K. Jason. Chicago: Swallow, 1973. Rpt. in *A Casebook on Anais Nin*, ed. Robert Zaller. New York: New American Library, 1974, pp. 113–31.

Barfield, Owen. *Saving the Appearances: A Study in Idolatry*. New York: Harcourt, Brace, n.d.

Barthes, Roland. *The Pleasure of the Text*. Trans. Richard Miller. New York: Hill & Wang, 1975.

Bendetti, Robert. "Metanaturalism: The Metaphorical Use of Environment in the Modern Theatre." *Chicago Review* 17, nos. 2 and 3: 24–32.

Bergson, Henri. *Matter and Memory*. Trans. Nancy Margaret Paul and W. Scott Palmer. London: Allen & Unwin, 1911.

Bettelheim, Bruno. *The Uses of Enchantment: The Meaning and Importance of Fairy Tales*. New York: Vintage, 1977.

Brée, Germaine. "The Strange World of Beckett's 'grands articules.' " Trans. Margaret Guiton. In *Samuel Beckett Now*, ed. Melvin J. Friedman. Chicago: University of Chicago Press, 1970, pp. 73–87.

Breton, André. *Manifestoes of Surrealism*. Trans. Richard Seaver and Helen R. Lane. Ann Arbor: University of Michigan Press, 1972.

Brown, Norman O. *Life against Death: The Psychoanalytical Meaning of History*. Middletown, Conn.: Wesleyan University Press, 1970.

——. *Love's Body*. New York: Vintage, 1966.

Carroll, William. "Nabokov's Signs and Symbols." In *A Book of Things about Vladimir Nabokov* ed. Carl R. Proffer. Ann Arbor: Ardis, 1974, pp. 203–17.

Clark, Orville. "Anais Nin: Studies in the New Erotology." Paper for a symposium for Anais Nin, 1972. Rpt. in *A Casebook on Anais Nin*, ed. Robert Zaller. New York: New American Library, 1974, pp. 101–11.

Coatzee, J. M. "Samuel Beckett's *Lessness:* An Exercise in Decomposition." *Computers and the Humanities* 7 (1973): 195–198.

Coe, Richard. *Samuel Beckett*. New York: Grove Press, 1970.

Cohn, Ruby. *Samuel Beckett: The Comic Gamut*. New Brunswick, N. J.: Rutgers University Press, 1962.

Corcoran, D. W. J. *Pattern Recognition*. Middlesex, England: Penguin, 1971.

Driver, Tom F. "Beckett by the Madeleine." *Columbia University Forum* 4 (summer 1961): 21–25.

Duffy, Martha. "I Have Never Seen a More Lucid, More Lonely, Better Balanced Mad Mind than Mine." *Time*, 23 May 1969, pp. 82–83.

Eliopulos, James. *Samuel Beckett's Dramatic Language*. The Hague: Mouton, 1975.

English, Priscilla. "An Interview with Anaïs Nin." *New Woman*, Dec. 1971. Rpt. in *A Casebook on Anaïs Nin*, ed. Robert Zaller. New York: New American Library, 1974, pp. 185–97.

Evans, Oliver. *Anaïs Nin*. Carbondale: Southern Illinois University Press, 1968.

Field, Andrew. *Nabokov: His Life in Art*. Boston: Little, Brown, 1967.

Fletcher, John. *Samuel Beckett's Art*. London: Chatto & Windus, 1967.

Freeman, Barbara. "A Dialogue with Anaïs Nin." *Chicago Review* 24 (1973): 29–35.

Grant, John E. "Imagination Dead?" *James Joyce Quarterly* 8 (1971): 336–62.

Greiner, Mechtilt Meijer. "Anaïs Nin." *Synthèses* 283/284 (1970): 75–77.

Hartman, Geoffrey H. "The Fate of Reading." In his *The Fate of Reading and Other Essays*. Chicago: University of Chicago Press, 1975.

Hinz, Evelyn J. *The Mirror and the Garden: Realism and Reality in the Writings of Anaïs Nin*. New York: Harcourt Brace Jovanovich, 1973.

Housman, A. E. *The Name and Nature of Poetry*. The Leslie Stephen Lecture, Cambridge, England, 9 May 1933. New York: Macmillan, 1933.

Howard, Richard. "A Note on *S/Z*." In *S/Z*, by Roland Barthes. New York: Hill and Wang, 1974.

Iser, Wolfgang. *The Implied Reader: Patterns of Communication in Prose Fiction from Bunyan to Beckett*. Baltimore: Johns Hopkins University Press, 1974.

James, D. G. "Metaphor and Symbol." In *Metaphor and Symbol*, ed. L. C. Knights and Basil Cottle. Proceedings of the Twelfth Symposium of the Colston Research Society, 28–31 March 1960. London: Butterworths, 1960, pp. 95–103.

Kenner, Hugh. *A Homemade World: The American Modernist Writers*. New York: William Morrow and Co., 1975.

Lee, L. L. *Vladimir Nabokov*. Boston: Twayne, 1976.

Mason, Bobbie Ann. *Nabokov's Garden: A Guide to "Ada."* Ann Arbor: Ardis, 1974.

McEvilly, Wayne "The Two Faces of Death in Anais Nin's *Seduction of the Minotaur*." *The New Mexico Quarterly*, winter-spring 1969, pp. 179–92. Rpt. as the afterword to *Seduction of the Minotaur* by Anais Nin. Chicago: Swallow, 1961, pp. 137–52.

Nelson, Cary. *The Incarnate Word: Literature as Verbal Space*. Urbana: University of Illinois Press, 1973.

O'Hara, J. D. "About Structure in *Malone Dies*." In *Twentieth Century Interpretations of "Molloy," "Malone Dies," "The Unnamable,"* ed. J. D. O'Hara. Englewood Cliffs, N. J.: Prentice-Hall, 1970, pp. 62–70.

———. "Beckett Piece by Piece." *The Nation*, 19 Feb. 1977, pp. 216–17, 219.

Paz, Octavio. *The Bow and the Lyre*. Trans. Ruth L. C. Simms. New York: McGraw-Hill, 1975.

Richard, Jean-Pierre. *Littérature et Sensation*. Paris: Editions du Seuil, 1954.

Robinson, Michael. *The Long Sonata of the Dead: A Study of Samuel Beckett*. New York: Grove Press, 1969.

Salehar, Anna Maria. "Nabokov's *Gift*: An Apprenticeship in Creativity." In *A Book of Things about Vladimir Nabokov*, ed. Carl R. Proffer. Ann Arbor: Ardis, 1974, pp. 70–83.

Sartre, Jean-Paul. *Being and Nothingness: An Essay on Phenomenological Ontology*. Trans. Hazel E. Barnes. New York: Washington Square Press, 1966.

Seaver, Richard, intro. and ed. *I Can't Go On, I'll Go On: A Selection from Samuel Beckett's Work*. New York: Grove Press, 1976.

Solomon, Philip H. *The Life after Birth: Imagery in Samuel Beckett's Trilogy*. University, Miss.: Romance Monographs, 1975.

Starke, John O. *The Literature of Exhaustion: Borges, Nabokov and Barth.* Durham, N. C.: Duke University Press, 1974.

Straus, Erwin. *The Primary World of the Senses: A Vindication of Sense Experience.* Trans. Jacob Needham. New York: Free Press, 1963.

Szanto, George. *Narrative Consciousness: Structure and Perception in the Fiction of Kafka, Beckett, and Robbe-Grillet.* Austin: University of Texas Press, 1972.

Tennyson, Alfred Lord. *The Poetic and Dramatic Works of Alfred Lord Tennyson.* Boston: Houghton, Mifflin, 1898.

Wilcher, Robert. " 'What's it meant to mean?': An Approach to Beckett's Theatre." *Critical Quarterly* 18 (summer 1976): 9−37.

INDEX

WORKS BY SAMUEL BECKETT

WORKS BY VLADIMIR NABOKOV

WORKS BY ANAIS NIN